How to be a *Lady* in God's Kingdom

How to be a *Lady* in God's Kingdom

DR. JOYCE SHELTON
With LYNN ERHORN

Lilyfield Publishing

How to be a *Lady* in God's Kingdom
Copyright © 2012 by Joyce Shelton
ISBN: 146641491X
ISBN-13: 978-1466414914

Lilyfield Publishing is an imprint of Fine Tune Services, LLC (Jacksonville, FL)

Scripture quotations, unless otherwise noted, are taken from the New King James
Version. Copyright © 1982 by Thomas Nelson, Inc. Used by permission.
Scripture quotations marked (TLB) are taken from The Living Bible, copyright ©
1971 by Tyndale House Publishers. Used by permission of Tyndale House
Publishers, Inc., Carol Stream, Illinois 60188. All rights reserved.

Lilyfield Publishing
PO Box 32113
Jacksonville, FL 32237
lilyfieldbooks@finetuneme.com

Cover Photograph: Michelle Arnold
Cover Design: Lynn Erhorn
Printed in the United States of America

DEDICATION

Above all, I give thanks and praise
and dedicate this book to my glorious
Heavenly Father
who loves His Ladies so.

CONTENTS

FOREWORD

Dr. Joyce Shelton has had a lot to do with my development as a minister, as a woman of faith, and now, as a lady. In the six years I have been privileged to know her, Joyce has been a living example of what the Bible encourages us to be: Full of mercy, deeply concerned for the brokenhearted, encouraging to others, and constantly willing to put her beliefs into action. Her Women of Excellence Ministry was already thriving in its tenth year when we met. I had recently moved from New York to Florida, arriving with a recent "Post Traumatic Stress Syndrome" diagnosis because I had endured a year that included four family deaths, a hysterectomy, and a move to a part of the country that was unfamiliar to me. Clearly, I wasn't at my best!

I was referred to Joyce for some Christian counseling and we accomplished some great healing in the short time I sat under her care in this capacity. Her gift of mercy, countenance of motherly concern, and strength of prayer warfare quickly helped me to arrive at the comment that ended our counseling relationship: "I don't have time to be broken." Fortunately, that comment also heralded the beginning of a precious friendship!

Very soon after that, Joyce hand selected about twenty-one people to participate in a class she was offering to complete her doctorate thesis. The subject was "Christian Facilitator's Training for Support Group Leadership," and I was surprised to be among those she invited. As it turned out, over three quarters of the students were selected from among Joyce's current or previous counseling clients. Within three months of completing the training, we were all put right to work helping to facilitate break-out groups for her regular classes in Christian living.

I mention this because I want you, dear reader, to know the heart of the lady who has written this love letter to you in the form of a book. Joyce lifts hearts, raises up ladies, and gently builds up leaders from among those who thought they could not benefit others. I can tell you first-hand that she strives to live out every word that she has penned and is engaged in the daily ministry of helping ladies like you do the same. With Joyce as my chief cheerleader, I went on to teach classes of my own, form a ministry, become a Christian Life Coach and Certified Pastoral Counselor. It has been a privilage to humbly accept the honor of working on this book with her. If you allow her to show you what God says about who you are in Christ Jesus, what He wants from your relationship with Him, and what He created you to become, I promise you will be richly blessed.

The initial request for my participation in this book was as an editor, since I have some experience writing and publishing. Along the way, Joyce's passion infected me and I found myself partnering with her in a much more intimate way, sometimes almost entirely rewriting a chapter in order to bring out the complete message I knew was in her heart. The project naturally evolved into something much more than an editing effort, and Joyce graciously invited me to share in the authorship. As honored as I am, I want you to know this book comes from Joyce's heart and from her faithful obedience to the Holy Spirit's inspiration. She wrote it and I consider it hers. To have been a part of the process and to have been given a voice where I felt strongly about a topic has made us better friends and has made me a better lady, for sure!

The pages that follow will always point you to the written Word of God as the highest authority. They will inspire you, encourage you, and sometimes challenge you. If you encounter areas of your life that need some work as you read, take heart! You are precious in God's sight and in ours, and we are praying for you and rooting for you!

We invite you to get to know us and our ministries better by visiting Dr. Joyce at her website (http://www.woeministry.com) or me at mine (http://www.perissosonline.org). May you mount up with wings like eagles as you embrace the message of this book!

Lynn Erhorn
Certified Pastoral Counselor
Perissos Resources, Inc.

PREFACE

As a Pastoral Counselor and a Director of Women of Excellence Ministry, I discovered that, at their core, my clients and students were simply seeking a working understanding of how to live a godly life. As I wrote this book, I felt the need to gather the best wisdom and materials I had used in countless sessions with women who were dealing with brokenheartedness, lack of truth, and reliance on their own soulish solutions. My precious Ladies were asking the same questions out of their need to be taught the deeper meaning of God's Word and how to apply it to their circumstances. Many of these women truly desired to walk in righteousness, yet were unsure of where the boundaries of God's laws and commandments belonged when lifted out of the Bible and laid down alongside their own struggles. As you read this book, keep in mind that God desires for you to seek Him first, placing your focus upon Him in a trusting relationship, then your righteousness will be added unto you (Matt 6:33).

It has been my pleasure to search for the truth of God's Word during my Christian walk and I am now passing the wisdom and understanding I've accumulated on to you. Having been raised in a spiritually bankrupt environment without the influence of the Word has given me a heart for each and every one of you and is the primary motivation that led me to this mission. My intent for you is that you will come to know what spiritual truths are available in exchange for the lies you have believed. My own experience revealed to me that, as I discovered and embraced the truth, it never failed to set me free from burdensome issues. My life as a Lady in God's Kingdom has been an ongoing process of restoration to God's peace, joy and the ability to love myself and others in a new manner, previously unfamiliar to me but wonderful and welcome when it arrived. I seek now to equip you with the same truth that so richly blessed and changed my life completely.

Helping others has been my life's work since meeting the Lord in early 1991. God has entrusted me with the privilege of helping many other women receive godly revelation and spiritual maturity. What a fulfilling privilege this has been to hold another's hand and walk with her through hard times and trials. This book was conceived out of a desire to leave a lasting legacy to Ladies everywhere who desired to know the truth and it grew up out of a challenge from my prayer partner, Connie Demetriou, to write it. Connie encouraged me chapter by chapter as the Lord pointed out to me nearly 50 virtues that described the distinctive characteristics of Ladies which ultimately became the complete outline for this book. I am so thankful for Connie and her devotion to inspire me through this process.

Lynn Erhorn joined the project when I began my search for an editor. Her years of experience writing and editing helped make this book come alive. Together, we narrowed the 19 chapters down to 12 and massaged the sentences until it finally looked like a real book. During our collaboration, I frequently told her, "Lynn, you are taking my lemons and making lemonade!" With a smile, she would always respond, "You already have lemonade. I'm just adding some sugar!" Lynn's skill and depth of knowledge of God's Word helped to bring out the truth on a deeper level than I ever imagined. I am very thankful for her willing partnership.

Thank you Lord for this unique calling and the ability to carry out the duties you have asked. I have enjoyed this walk and the occasions of experiencing or witnessing every miracle and healing touch you demonstrated to each Lady you placed in my care. You have given all three of us Ladies a heart to see hurting women healed of all their offenses, wounds, and victimizations. It excites our spirits to share the truth of Your love with them, Jesus.

A Word of Encouragement to the Lady Reader

As women, we must keep in mind that we are uniquely different from men in our virtues. We don't have to compete with them or imitate their manly ways. We simply have to engage in being a Lady and allow our men to be all that they were designed to be. It grieves me when I see a woman trying to cross these invisible lines in competition, seeking to make it in a man's position while wearing Prada shoes, losing all of her Lady-like qualities to pursue a path that God did not plan for her. This is a dangerous place to be. You weren't made to cast away your beautiful qualities and distinctions—they are a gift from God to embrace as your very own. Rather, stand for the truth of God's Word and take ownership of your virtues! I encourage each one of you to BE A LADY and glorify God by expressing fully what He made you to be.

Now, to you Ladies who are seeking a full measure of truth: You will find the truth if you simply search for it in God's Word. It is our Lord and Savior's desires to influence you with His everlasting love that will change your life forever. He is awaiting your attention to the pages of His love letters to you. So pursue the truth and it will serve you richly. Find the fullness of it and you will never be the same. Through it, you will be the mirrored image of Jesus.

ACKNOWLEDGMENTS

My heartfelt thanks to these special people, who were so supportive
during the writing of this book:

Lynn Erhorn who was my chief editor and collaborator.
Your dedication of many hours spent writing, editing and providing
insight was outstanding.
Thank you for your time and love.

Connie Demetriou who spent time chatting and praying for this book.
You have been my prayer partner, friend, cheerleader and encourager.

Dana Preston who kindly offered to serve as preliminary editor.
The hours you spent bore wonderful fruit. You are such a blessing.
Mum's the word on the hilarious mistakes that I made.

Colleen Peters who gave her time reading each page to me out-loud so
I could hear what I had written.
Thanks Colleen, for your devotion.

Michel Oesterreicher who gave her time and expertise reading and
directing the spiritual accuracy of this book.

Michelle Arnold, photographer and Jill Hawthorne, cover photo
model, who gave us this beautiful cover. I'm grateful for their
expressed delight in being a part of this project.
Thank you both for your devoted time and talents.

Carrie Simpson and Shelly Pike, whose valuable perspective on the
purity and femininity chapters helped tremendously.

Rev. Charles Shelton, my husband, who has always encouraged me to
follow God in all that I do.
Thank you for enduring all the long hours of writing.

My children and their spouses whose love is always there.
Traci & Mike, Travis & Aimee,
Charles & Christy, Charlene & Anthony, and Thomas & Leigh,
you are deeply appreciated.

Rev. Steve McCoy who has imparted to me the Christian principles of
life through his sermon messages at Beaches Chapel Church on
Sundays and Wednesdays since 1991.

Deena DuBose whom I have respected for many years for following
God's voice and direction.
Thank you Deena for introducing me
to the world of writing for the glory of God.
Your encouragement and friendship has been
a priceless jewel in my life.

My clients and students with whom I practiced the messages
in these pages throughout the years.

My prayer warriors:
Debbie Mainville, Ann Dillard, and Dora Escudero
for their vigilance and constant covering.

INTRODUCTION

This book is written for the Lady in pursuit of the knowledge and wisdom she needs to live a devoted Christian life. Let's face it Ladies, the world around us offers many choices but we're not always certain what the godly choice should be. We sometimes need the truth revealed to us in relevant ways in order to choose as God wills. This book eliminates the confusion of decision-making and explains key godly principles to guide you in your daily life. Equipped with the Biblical perspective provided in these pages, a Lady no longer has to teeter on the fence trying to decide what is right or wrong. The closer you follow the plan God has for your life, the more you will look like the radiant, healthy, and powerfully effective Lady you were created to be!

The Bible tells us in John 8:31-32, *"If you abide in My word, you are My disciples indeed and you shall know the truth, and the truth shall make you free."* This means that if you are determined to be a student of God's Word you will discover the truth—this is His promise! Each chapter that follows studies a particular attribute of a Lady's total being and puts it in clear perspective, helping her to determine God's will for her life. Together, we will endeavor to remove the doubts, settle the inner arguments, and embrace the genuine truth for making godly decisions. We'll place our focus on faith and dependent trust in God. If you approach these pages with your heart open to hear the truth that frees you, there is a good chance you will be transformed in the process.

Every endeavor starts with a decision.
Choice, not chance, determines the outcome.

How to Use This Book

Where the opportunity presented itself, I have inserted questions and left space for you to write in your own answers as you read. Give these your most honest response. Just write from your heart's depth. Also, at the end of each chapter are six discussion questions to use individually or in a small group setting. It is often helpful if you share your answers with an accountability partner or in a small group devoted to emotional and spiritual healing. (See Appendix A for instructions on starting your own small support group.)

You are encouraged to prayerfully contemplate your answers to the discussion questions before addressing them with someone else. Write your most honest responses, but you may choose to keep some things to yourself in a group setting. This is fine. As you form trust within your group, you may become more comfortable telling the whole truth about your circumstances. Wherever you hide pain in your heart, you will eventually need to break the silence in a safe environment in order to heal. If your group doesn't seem like an ideal place to explore that path, I encourage you to seek out a Christian counselor, perhaps bringing your answers to these questions as a jumping off point for your conversations. Also, pray as you read and answer these questions. You will want God to be involved with you in your responses.

God is not asking for perfect righteousness in your answers. He knows how to bring that about in you. Rather, He is seeking to possess your heart. He wants you to surrender your every thought, desire, and emotion to Him, bringing your heart into oneness with His.

Significantly, the prayers at the end of each chapter are prayers of deliverance. If you truly want to renounce and surrender your struggles, these prayers include words of confession, forgiveness, and repentance which can bring the immediate change you are seeking, if you pray them with faith from your heart.

God has a message of love to share with every Lady who wants to grow in the grace and knowledge of His Word. So, are you ready to learn more about just how much you are loved and about the promises available to you? "Yes," you say? Well then, sit back, breathe deeply, and take the next step on the path to discovering what it means to be a Lady in God's Kingdom.

May the Lord bless you with His agape love as you read!

SECTION I

A LADY'S
SPIRITUAL FOUNDATION

"To the elect Lady…whom I love in truth…
And now I plead with you, Lady,
not as though I wrote a new commandment to you,
but that which we have had from the beginning:
that we love one another.
This is love,
that we walk according to His commandments"
(2 John 1:5-6)

1

HER COMMITMENT

A LADY COMMITS HER LIFE TO THE LORD.
SHE CHOOSES TO BELIEVE WITH ALL HER HEART.

What is it that we Ladies are seeking in life? Is it the status of being elite, the appearance of elegance, the riches of wealth, or the power to rule? Maybe you are seeking a clear understanding of your worth, or the purpose for which you were born? What path would you venture down in your quest to be a Lady? The Bible says: *"For where your treasure is, there your heart will be also"* (Matt 6:21). In other words, if your choice is to be powerful, rich, elite, and in charge, this is what your heart will choose to depend upon in times of need. God is letting us in on a little secret here: Where you aim your heart is exactly where you will land! Plainly put, your decisions and choices will determine your destinations in life.

Ask yourself: Am I looking for heavenly principles to shape and direct my life or am I treasuring things that won't last or accumulate any eternal value? In answering that question, have you discovered if you need to aim at a new target and find a new path that will take you into God's territory? If your heart's desire is to become the Lady God is calling you to be then there is solid truth ahead to help you fulfill that dream. Your quest for spiritual excellence will connect you to the greatness of a personal and transforming relationship with God. So, let's get started without delay!

Commitment to Becoming a Lady

In the book of Proverbs, The Virtuous Woman possesses a worth more valuable than precious gems. She is a woman of strength and dignity whose words are wise and who makes kindness her priority. I want you to know that developing into a Virtuous Woman is a wonderful goal for any Lady to aspire to, however there is an even greater goal with a tremendous prize at your fingertips. You can become all that your heavenly Father desires you to be with the help of the Bible bringing all things into perspective. In those lovingly inspired pages, you will encounter the complete truth and not just a portion of the truth. These biblical riches of truth can be your reward in wisdom if embraced and applied to your life.

Your biblical development into God's precious Lady is a life-long journey, which you walk hand-in-hand with God. Your partnership in this expedition will yield peace, patience, goodness, kindness, faith, surrender, repentance, forgiveness, and many more virtuous attributes, all of which you collect along the way like treasure.

God's intention and deep desire is to see Himself reflected in you like a mirror. His promise is this: As you follow His word of truth He will change you so that His light will shine through you to others. Wherever you are today in your walk with God, you have the opportunity to be transformed as God performs His glorious work in you. Don't be afraid of losing yourself to become God's precious Lady. In fact, Jesus tells us that we must lose our life in order to gain it (Mark 8:35). That means you need to make a decision and then stick with it. Let me offer you these seven beliefs that represent the basic building blocks for you as a Lady. Your commitment to the journey starts with these steps.

1. **A Lady believes Jesus is her Savior and Lord.**
   "For God so loved the world that He gave His only begotten Son, that whoever believes in Him should not perish but have everlasting life" (John 3:16).

   The first step of your commitment is accepting Jesus as your Savior and Lord. Receiving Christ as your Savior is called Salvation or "being born again" which means that you trust Jesus enough to surrender your life to Him. Receiving your Salvation brings the surety of knowing that when you die, your soul will live on with Christ eternally. Salvation is accomplished by saying a simple prayer of surrender and an act of honesty in your heart that you want Jesus to be your Savior.

The meaning of being "born again" is to be given a godly Spirit. It is not a physical birth like your first birth, but you are being re-birthed as an entirely new creation with a clean slate, indwelt with God's Holy Spirit. (The next chapter discusses Salvation in greater detail.)

Making Jesus your Lord is moving from receiving Him as your Savior into a moment-to-moment relationship with Him as your Lord. Salvation is the initial commitment but Lordship is the continual devotion. He desires for His Ladies to unite in relationship with Him all the days of their lives.

If a Lady can build a strong cathedral with Christ as her Savior and Lord, by permitting Jesus to be her solid and stable foundation, she will not live in a crumbling tower with need for many repairs and maintenance. She eagerly embraces her Lord and lives in the prosperity of an honest and open relationship with Him which proves and stands the test of time.

Have you made Jesus your Savior and Lord?

_____

2. **A Lady believes the Bible is the truth.**
"For this wonderful news, the message that God wants to save us, has been given to us just as it was to those who lived in the time of Moses... For only we who believe God can enter into his place of rest" (Heb 4:2-3 TLB).

Believing the Bible is at the beginning of a Lady's spiritual development. The Bible is an inerrant book, which means it is without flaw or mistake. God wrote His word through a chosen few whom He inspired and His message has been preserved through the centuries for each one of us to live by. It is intended to be your owner's manual and it has a valid reference for every situation you might encounter in your entire lifetime.

A Lady's life can be guided by every scripture passage if she believes and follows the truth of each written Word. As you engage your faith by reading the Bible, you will be stabilized by its truth, becoming confident in who you are – adding to your virtues and establishing your solid character in Christ Jesus. It is only a matter of believing and the Bible will unfold the truth and sustain you each day.

Do you believe the Bible is the full truth for your life?

_____

3. **A Lady believes in being honest.**

"Be honest in your estimate of yourselves, measuring your value by how much faith God has given you" (Rom 12:3 TLB).

Being honest with yourself and God is the third step to being a Lady. Sometimes, you might find yourself tempted to hide behind lies, especially if your truth has been a broken heart, shame from your past, or a soul that clings to anger, resentment, guiltiness, or rejection. When you choose Salvation and a life with Christ, you surrender all of the devastations and destructions of your heart to receive His healing, forgiveness, cleansing, and refreshing as you journey with Him. God brings to light all things that are hidden and stuffed away in darkness giving you an open opportunity to be truthful with Him. It is a brave process, one that a courageous Lady truthfully indulges in by saying, *"Search my heart, Oh, Lord"* (Psa 139). A Lady in God's Kingdom truly desires to be open, sharing her heart in honesty with her Lord and herself.

Are you openly honest with God?

_____

4. **A Lady believes in being humble.**

"Therefore humble yourselves under the mighty hand of God, that He may exalt you in due time, casting all your care upon Him, for He cares for you" (1 Peter 5:6-7).

Biblical humility is not a belittling of oneself but an exalting or praising of others, especially God. A humble Lady removes herself as the center of all focus and places the spotlight on others, rather than herself. Humbleness brings her pride to a halt and delights her soul in the purposes of God. She carries herself with modesty, meekness, and an unassuming nature. The Bible says, *"God gives His grace to the humble"* (1 Pet 5:5). It is only through the grace of humbleness that a Lady can devote her life to serving like Christ served. As she models Christ's character of humbleness, it gives her an opportunity to impart to others, her reverence of Christ.

Do you believe in being humble?

✎ _____

5. **A Lady believes she needs to forgive.**

"And whenever you stand praying, if you have anything against anyone, forgive him that your Father in heaven may also forgive you your trespasses. But if you do not forgive, neither will your Father in heaven forgive your trespasses" (Mark 11:25-26).

Forgiveness brings new freedom to a Lady when she learns to humbly forgive herself of her own sins, weaknesses and shortcomings. It opens the door for her to forgive others. She knows that it is a command from God to forgive that must be carried out in obedience to His will. By asking her Lord to help her forgive the offenses of others, she places these accumulated concerns into Christ's hands and walks away, leaving all unforgiveness at the foot of His cross. Then, as her delicate heart is unburdened, she is set free to do as God asks and go as He calls her. After receiving forgiveness, her heavenly Father brings new faith to her heart – exactly what she needs for the destiny ahead. (Chapter 9 offers more on forgiveness.)

Do you believe that you need to forgive yourself and others?

✎ _____

6. **A Lady believes she needs to repent.**

"Repent therefore and be converted, that your sins may be blotted out, so that times of refreshing may come from the presence of the Lord" (Acts 3:19).

Repenting involves turning away from sinning and turning toward righteousness. The term signifies "to have another mind," in other words, to change your opinion or purpose with regard to sin (any thought, word, or deed that is contrary to God's will and character). The Lord desires for us to lead a righteous life after accepting Him as our Savior. A Lady makes a conscious, moral separation, and a personal decision to forsake sin and to enter into fellowship with God. She feels remorse for her previous poor choices and expresses them to Him. She also has a new understanding of who God is and the preciousness of His eternal commitment to her at all times – especially when she misses the mark of righteousness. She believes it is necessary on a regular basis to repent, when she realizes that she has disobeyed her Lord.

Do you take time to repent frequently?

_____

7. A Lady believes she needs to pray.

"If My people who are called by My name will humble themselves, and pray and seek My face, and turn from their wicked ways, then I will hear from heaven, and will forgive their sin and heal their land. Now My eyes will be open and My ears attentive to prayer made in this place" (2 Chron 7:14-15).

A Lady acknowledges her need to communicate with God through prayer. She is assured through the Bible that God is a personal God, active and living, all-knowing, all-wise, and all-powerful, who can hear her prayers and help her. She builds her prayer-life on the cornerstone of Christ's work on the cross and the tender promises of her loving heavenly Father. Her prayers spring out of a desire to agree with God's plans for her life as she places her faith in Him to guide her. Hebrews 11:6 says, *"But without faith it is impossible to please Him, for he who comes to God must believe that He is, and that He is a rewarder of those who diligently seek Him."* Through her devotion to prayer, she has new freedom from anxiety and worry of the future.

Do you believe that you need to frequently seek God in prayer?

_____

Now that we have established these seven beliefs that make up a Lady's commitment to God, you will need to know how to apply them to your daily life. The chapters ahead will give you a clear picture of the virtues and characteristic traits that God designed specifically with all Ladies in mind. My prayer is that they will give you a better understanding of God's Word and bring you refreshed hope and determination for the development of your spiritual life.

Keep in mind that a Lady is devoted to God in every decision she makes. This isn't a ball-and-chain prison of a relationship. It is the most freeing commitment you will ever make. So, if there is any hesitation lingering in you, I say throw off those chains that bind you and let's go collect those treasures!

Prayer: A Lady's Commitment

Dear Precious Lord,

I come before You today surrendered to Your will and guidance in my life. I only want what You want for me. I lay aside my "self" and take upon Your righteous ways written in Your precious Bible. I proclaim the truth of Your Holy Word to be imparted and manifested through me. I receive every promise You have for me to encounter including my belief that Jesus is my Lord, the Word is my truth, I have been given the blessing of honesty, humbleness, forgiveness, and repentance, with a willingness to seek You at all times in prayer. Help me Lord to become the Lady that you so desire for me to be. Take my unrighteousness and turn it into the virtuousness that You have proclaimed that I shall become. I want to experience those days of holiness, truthfulness, and righteous decision-making. Give me wisdom and help me to embrace Your endeavors within me, all the days of my life.

I call You my Lord and identify myself as Your child. As a child, I shall seek You as my source knowing that You are the author and finisher of my faith. Come Lord, Jesus as I worship You in Spirit and in truth. Change me into Your image of righteousness with a new identity, reputation, integrity and countenance. I praise You for who you are and give You the glory that You deserve to hear from my lips. Direct my life's path. In Jesus' holy name I pray. Amen.

Group Discussion: Your Commitment

1. Have you been challenged in being a real Lady in the areas of honesty, humility, forgiveness, repentance and/or prayer? Reveal your struggles in these areas.

2. What information can you share regarding being a Lady in God's presence? How has your behavior, actions, speech or thoughts been pleasing to Him?

3. Reviewing this last year of your life, what is the first thing you might do differently to become more of a Lady in God's eyes?

4. Talk about your current challenges with being open and honest about your heart issues. Are there things you don't trust God to know about yourself?

5. Which of the seven belief commitments are you already applying in your life? How would you use them to encourage others in being a Lady in God's Kingdom?

6. Share your joy about wanting to be a Lady. Are you willing to exchange your sorrows and disappointments for what God has waiting to give you today? What would you exchange?

*"If you confess with your mouth the Lord Jesus
and believe in your heart that God has raised Him from the dead,
you will be saved.
For with the heart one believes unto righteousness,
and with the mouth confession is made unto salvation."
(Romans 10:9-10)*

HER SALVATION

A LADY MAKES THE CHOICE TO ACCEPT JESUS AS HER SAVIOR.
SHE DESIRES TO BE ONE WITH HER BELOVED.

You can find what the deepest part of your heart has been searching for simply by accepting Jesus as your Savior and then getting to know Him in a greater way as your Lord. If you haven't already experienced this greatest of all joys, dear Lady, know that receiving your Salvation in Him will reveal your true worth and bring you the peace and contentment you have not yet been able to find. Fulfillment, wholeness, and stability are all within your grasp as you uncover the mysteries behind Jesus' love and plan for your life. He is always waiting for you to accept His invitation, but the decision is yours. Even if you have made Jesus your Savior, I urge you to resist any temptation to skip this chapter. There is always something to learn about making Him *Lord*. Let's look closer at what Salvation means.

What Is Salvation?

Salvation can best be understood as your deliverance *from* the dilemma of sin *to* a place of conscious righteousness, coupled with the free gift of eternal life starting right now and continuing in Heaven. You can look forward to forgiveness of any and all sins, a new life, and restored fellowship with your heavenly Father God. From the moment you answer His call, you begin an eternity basking in the promises He made available to anyone who will receive them. *"Truly, truly, I say to you, he who hears My word, and believes Him who sent Me, has eternal life , and does not come into judgment, but has passed out of death into life"* (John 5:24).

The Decision

We all have a decision to make concerning our Salvation and eternal life before we leave this earth. You can say, "Yes" or "No" according to *your* will. Jesus offers you this free gift of Salvation; all you have to do is decide whether you want to receive eternal life and the removal of your sins as you claim Him as your Savior. God loves each one of us so much allowing us to freely choose to accept Jesus as our Savior. He does not force us—but wants us to willingly come to Him. Ephesians 2:4-6 tells us, *"But God is so rich in mercy; he loved us so much that even though we were spiritually dead and doomed by our sins, he gave us back our lives again when he raised Christ from the dead"* (TLB).

What stands in the way of receiving Salvation and therefore relationship with God? Our sins! God is perfect and because He is, He cannot bear our imperfection of sin. We as human beings all sin. The word simply means "missing the mark." We all miss the mark of God's perfect will for us somewhere in our lives. This sin nature was inherited from Adam and Eve because they disobeyed and "missed the mark." They chose their own will, not God's, setting the stage for all of the generations to come. Romans 3:23 reminds us: *"For all have sinned and fall short of the glory of God."* You may not think you have fallen *as short* as some others you know, but you are not off the hook as far as sin is concerned unless you accept and receive forgiveness through Salvation in Christ. *"No one is good—no one in all the world is innocent. No one has ever really followed God's paths or even truly wanted to. Everyone has turned away; all have gone wrong. No one anywhere has kept on doing what is right; not one,"* confirms Romans 3:10-12 (TLB).

Sin is what separates us from God. It is so far from His nature, He cannot tolerate sin near Him and remain pure and perfect. This necessary distance from relationship with us grieves God's heart as any separation from a loved one would grieve yours. However, as our faithful Redeemer, God had a plan for our liberation. Since we cannot pay the price for our sins, He devised a way to allow Christ to pay this price on our behalf. The provision that restores your relationship with God is a meaningful decision from your heart to accept Jesus Christ as your Savior therefore receiving His free gift of Salvation and full forgiveness of your sins. Upon your acceptance of this gift you are united with God and a brand new relationship commences. Should your earthly life end without having made this essential decision of Salvation, you shall remain separated from God eternally. There must be a decision made from your heart and with your mouth. It would be a tragedy to fail to make your choice, considering the consequence of an eternity separated from the One who created you and loves you so much. If you have never made a decision to receive your free gift of Salvation, you can become God's Lady right now.

What a Lady Does To Receive Her Free Gift of Salvation.

1. **She Recognizes Her Status**
   A Lady acknowledges that she was and is a sinner.
   Romans 3:10 states, *"There is no person without sin."* In other words, we all make mistakes and we all sin against God. We were born into this sin-nature and will continue to "miss the mark" all throughout our lives. A Lady realizes she is not perfect in the eyes of God and there is great danger in remaining in that state.

2. **She Understands Her Dilemma**
   A Lady understands that her sin demands payment.
   The Bible says our sin results in death—physical, spiritual, and eternal. (Rom 6:23). In other words, Jesus went to the cross for you and for me to pay for sin that we were unable to pay ourselves. He took our place! What a great love! A Lady greatly understands that Jesus paid a debt that she could not pay.

3. **She Confesses Her Sin**
   A Lady chooses to confess her sin to God.
   A Lady acknowledges her need to confess (agree with God about) her sins. This lets God know that you know you are a sinner. When a Lady admits her sin and asks God's forgiveness, the amazing act of love Jesus did on the cross releases her from every sin forever. William Temple, Archbishop of Canterbury, is quoted as saying "I can contribute nothing to my own salvation, except the sin from which I need to be redeemed."

4. **She Receives Jesus**

A Lady receives Jesus' gift of Salvation.

The heart of the gospel is found in John 3:16: *"For God so loved the world that He gave His only begotten Son that whoever believes in Him should not perish but have everlasting life."* Please understand that His Salvation is a free gift. You can't earn it by being good enough or by doing good deeds for God. You simply have to choose to receive it. Think of it this way: If someone brings a beautifully wrapped gift into your home and sets it on your table, it belongs totally to you. But, if you never open it, you have not received it and you won't benefit from whatever treasure is inside. Romans 10:10 tells us, *"We believe with our hearts, and so we are made right with God. And we use our mouths to say that we believe, and so we are saved."* A Lady believes, and then accepts her gift of forgiveness of sin and Salvation through Jesus' sacrifice at the cross.

5. **She Surrenders to Jesus**

A Lady surrenders her life to God following Him all her days.

Surrendering means to give up your sinful life and yield to God's will and plan for your life. 2 Chronicles 30:8 tells us, *"Now do not be stiff-necked...but yield yourselves to the Lord."* It is also making the choice to turn away from sinning again, meaning to "repent" (turn away) from your sin. A Lady chooses to willingly make changes in her lifestyle in order to follow God and live out His incredible plan for her.

6. **She Thanks Jesus**

A Lady thanks Jesus for paying the price for her life.

A heart filled with gratitude is a natural response to Salvation. A Lady submits her thankfulness to her Lord knowing that He redeemed her life and saved her from eternal doom. It is a continual thankfulness that emanates from her forever. Psalm 100 is a song of thanksgiving. In verse 4, we are encouraged to *"Enter into His gates with thanksgiving and into His courts with praise. Be thankful to Him and bless His name."*

7. **She Shares Jesus**

A Lady shares her decision with others in celebration.

The resurrected Jesus gave these instructions to His disciples and to us today: *"Go, therefore, and make disciples of all the nations"* (Matt 28:19). A Lady celebrates the fact that God has taken habitation in her heart and will be with her from this moment on. She shares this celebration with others. Her life is to be a continual reflection of what God has done for her.

Your New Life

Receiving Salvation is the beginning of your new and eternal life. I urge you to make this decision now, since neither you nor I are guaranteed a tomorrow. It is a choice that you will never regret. So, decide today where you will spend eternity and clear away the doubt in your mind about your forgiveness and where your soul will go when you pass away. Today is your day to know your destiny for sure!

Prayer: A Lady's Salvation

If you desire to receive Christ as your Savior please pray this prayer from your heart and receive Him as your Redeemer and you will be eternally saved.

Dear Heavenly Father,

I pray and ask Jesus to come into my heart to be my personal Lord and Savior. I confess that I am a sinner. I ask that You forgive me and release me of all my sins by Your grace. I acknowledge that Jesus died on the cross at Calvary so I could have eternal life in Your heavenly Kingdom. I believe that Jesus was raised from the dead and He is seated at Your right hand. Oh, God, I accept this free gift of Eternal Life from You.

Thank you, Jesus, for paying the penalty for my sins and giving me a continued life in heaven with You. Please make me to be the person You created me to be. I only want Your will for my life now. Thank you for receiving me into Your Kingdom. Amen.

If you have just committed your life to Christ

Ladies, whether you are renewing your faith or committing for the first time to your life of Salvation, I celebrate with you this new relationship with your living God! It is the most important decision you have ever made in your entire life. I encourage you to join a church that teaches the Bible, to begin spending a few minutes every day praying to God and reading your Bible. Start with the Gospels of Matthew, Mark, Luke and John. These books tell you about the life and ministry of Jesus here on earth. I pray that you will follow Him and experience all the blessings He has for you in your journey ahead.

Group Discussion: Your Salvation

1. Did you know about the free gift of Salvation prior to this message? Have you heard the message and refused to accept it? Why?

2. Do you understand Salvation and being separated from God through your sins? What part still needs to be explained for you to understand?

3. Are you willing to receive the free gift of eternal life by saying the prayer? Why or why not?

4. When you said the Prayer of Salvation, did you mean it from your heart? Did you feel a softening of your heart at that time? What other feelings did you encounter?

5. Who would you like to tell that you have received the free gift of Salvation? Why? Was this an exciting moment for you to be saved?

6. Who would you like to see saved through Salvation and why?

*"Now your attitudes and thoughts must all be
constantly changing for the better.
Yes, you must be a new and different person,
holy and good.
Clothe yourself with this new nature."
(Ephesians 4:23-24 TLB)*

HER IDENTITY

When a Lady learns who she is in Christ she discovers a brand new person with new principles, truths and purposes. Her "old man" (Eph 4:23-24) passes away and her new identity is introduced bringing a fresh righteous standard, and a changed nature of holiness from within her spirit. This transformation is referred to as becoming a "new creation in Christ." 2 Corinthians 5:17-18 proclaims, *"If anyone is in Christ, he is a new creation; old things have passed away; behold, all things have become new."* Like the caterpillar changing into a butterfly, you are never the same again. You are made beautiful in Christ because your sin no longer covers up your beauty. Your earthly image of yourself based on your nationality, family heritage, relationships, possessions, job, or family status pales in comparison to your pristine new identity. Your likeness to Christ and your uniqueness as a child of God are your two new distinctive qualities.

Your new identity is an amazing metamorphosis. You are washed of all your sins, sanctified and made holy; justified and made acceptable by the Spirit of God now living in you. You have a new inheritance which includes security and significance in Christ. These are just some of the promises of God mentioned in the previous chapter. Are you exhilarated? Let's keep going, and discover together more of what Scripture says about your new identity.

♥ **You Are Chosen.** You are hand-picked by God. Ephesians 1:4 says, *"He chose us in Him* (hand-picked) *before the foundation of the world, that we should be holy and without blame before Him in love."* This means that you have been individually selected by God to be in relationship with Him, to take on His character and inherit and dwell in His kingdom. He also chose you to be holy and blameless in His sight. Wow, what a new you!

When you think about being individually picked by the coach of a team to play a game, don't you want to be picked first and not passed over until all the other players are chosen? What a delight to know that you are a wanted member, not just a third-string bench warmer hoping to get picked. You were purposefully chosen by God, from the very beginning. Of course, God's love is limitless and He chooses every one of His children for the team. However, the proper response of a Lady is to choose Him in return.

♥ **You Are Adopted.** You were specifically selected by God. Ephesians 1:5 says, *"Having predestined us* (decided beforehand) *to adoption* (selection) *as sons by Jesus Christ to Himself, according to the good pleasure of His will."* An adopted child comes with documents of commitment and declarations of rights and privileges from the court that assures equality of care with that of the natural born child. This process for the adoptive parents is deliberate, premeditated and intentional in commitment. This child is honored as a purposed child, one who is accepted and selected lovingly by the parents. Knowing that a Lady is adopted in God's Kingdom brings a warm-fuzzy feeling of comfort. Do you feel that way too, knowing that you were *deliberately* adopted by God?

♥ **You Are Made Heirs.** You are regarded by God as His child, meaning an heir in His family. 1 John 3:1 says, *"Behold what manner of love the Father has bestowed on us, that we should be called children (heirs) of God!"* Becoming an heir of great wealth, position, and power tickles my fancy. It is a delight to know that as a child of God, we have a great inheritance, filled with every blessing to promote our growth, wellbeing, and righteousness. Everything that Jesus inherited you and I have also inherited—the same benefits and promises. All things of God's Kingdom were inherited when we said the precious words of Salvation to believe in Jesus.

♥ **You Are Forgiven.** You are released by God from the debt accumulated by every sin. 1 John 1:9 says, *"If we confess our sins, He is faithful and just to forgive (release) us of our sins and to cleanse us from all unrighteousness."* God's desire and intention is to make sure that your sins do not interfere with your relationship with Him. Therefore, He forgives you of all your sins and releases you from the burden of each sin through Jesus paying the price once and for all. Your identity can rest on the assurance that your sins—past, present, and future—are completely wiped away. Isn't that a great feeling? You don't have to try to pay for them anymore. *"It is finished,"* says Jesus. *"I did it for you"* (John 19:30).

♥ **You Are Made Holy.** Colossians 1:21-22 affirms your position with God saying, *"And you, who once were alienated and enemies in your mind by wicked works, yet now He has reconciled in the body of His flesh through death, to present you holy, and blameless, and above reproach in His sight."* God removes all your blame and shame. You are now seen as sacred, innocent, and without disgrace, holy in God's sight. Knowing that you are blameless for all of your sinful ways can bring comfort and relief to your soul. To be made holy is to be set apart from the rest of the world for sacred use. We are holy because He is holy. Cleansed of sin, a Lady is now prepared to reflect God's character. She lives in this world, but she is no longer of this earthly world (John 15:19, 17:14).

My collaborator in this book, Lynn Erhorn, uses the exercise that follows in her Life Coaching ministry. It is adapted from a similar process described in Neil Anderson's "Christ Centered Therapy."[1] I believe it will help you gain a solid understanding of exactly who you are in the eyes of God and to see yourself the way He does. However, you may see yourself now, your true identity is in who you are because of what God has done in Christ to win you as His own!

Go ahead and fill it in now. Allow your heart to soar as you hear your Heavenly Father boast about how much He loves you! Then, permit yourself to write the statements under each Scripture in the same, loving light.

EXERCISE

WHO AM I IN CHRIST?

Instructions

The scriptures in this exercise are all taken from the NIV translation (unless otherwise noted). Please turn to them in your Bible to fill in the blanks. If you're using another version, simply fill in the blanks as closely as you can, making sure you understand what the Word is saying to you. Then, in the space beneath each scripture, write a brief statement of how this applies to you personally. Use the blank space after the very last question to write a 2-3 paragraph summary based on this exercise that describes who you are in Christ. The first one is completed for you as an example.

I Am Accepted In Christ

Yet to all who did receive him, to those who believed in his name, he gave the right to become **children** of God. *(John 1:12)*

I am a child of God.

I no longer call you servants, because a servant does not know his master's business. Instead, I have called you _____, for everything that I learned from my Father I have made known to you. *(John 15:15)*

Therefore, since we have been _____ through faith, we have peace with God through our Lord Jesus Christ. *(Romans 5:1)*

But whoever is united with the Lord is _____ in spirit. *(1 Corinthians 6:17)*

You were _____.
Therefore honor God with your bodies. *(1 Corinthians 6:20)*

Now you are the _____ of Christ, and each one of you
is a _____ of it. *(1 Corinthians 12:27)*

Paul, an apostle of Christ Jesus by the will of God, to the
_____ who are in Ephesus, and are faithful in Christ
Jesus. *(Ephesians 1:1 ESV)*

For he _____ in him before the creation of
the world to be holy and _____in his sight.
(Ephesians 1:4)

He predestined us for _____ through Jesus Christ,
in accordance with his pleasure and will. *(Ephesians 1:5)*

For through him we both have _____ to
the Father by one Spirit. *(Ephesians 2:18)*

For he has _____ us from the dominion of darkness
and brought us into the kingdom of the Son he loves, in whom we
have _____, the _____
of sins. *(Colossians 1: 13-14)*

For in Christ all the fullness of the Deity lives in bodily form, and in
_____ you have been brought to
_____. (Colossians 2:9-10)

I Am Secure In Christ

Therefore, there is now no condemnation for those who are in Christ
Jesus, because through Christ Jesus the law of the Spirit of life has
_____ me _____ from the law
of sin and death. (Romans 8:1-2)

And we know that in all things God _____ of those who
love him, who have been called according to his purpose. (Romans 8:28)

Who will bring any charge against those whom God has chosen? It is
God who justifies. Who then is the one who condemns?
_____ who died—more than that, who was raised to
life—is at the right hand of God and is also _____
for us. (Romans 8:33-34)

Who shall separate us from the _____?
Shall trouble or hardship or persecution or famine or nakedness or
danger or sword? For I am convinced that neither death nor life,
neither angels nor demons, neither the present nor the future, nor any
powers, neither height nor depth, nor anything else in all creation, will
be able to separate us from the _____
that is in Christ Jesus our Lord. (Romans 8:35, 38-39)

Now it is God who makes both us and you stand firm in Christ. He _____ us, set his _____ on us, and put his Spirit in our hearts as a deposit, _____ what is to come. *(2 Corinthians 1:21-22)*

Being confident of this, that he who began a good work in you will carry it on to _____ until the day of Christ Jesus. *(Philippians 1:6)*

But our _____ is in heaven. And we eagerly await a Savior from there, the Lord Jesus Christ, who, by the power that enables him to bring everything under his control, will transform our lowly bodies so that they will be like his glorious body. *(Philippians 3:20-21)*

For you died, and your life is now _____ in God. *(Colossians 3:3)*

But because of his great love for us, God, who is rich in mercy, made us _____ even when we were dead in transgressions—it is by grace you have been saved. *(Ephesians 2:4-5)*

For the Spirit God gave us does not make us timid, but gives us _____, _____ and _____. *(2 Timothy 1:7)*

Let us then approach God's throne of grace with _____, so that we may receive _____ and find _____ to help us in our time of need. *(Hebrews 4:16)*

You, dear children, _____ and have overcome them, because the one who is in you is _____ than the one who is in the world. *(1 John 4:4)*

We know that anyone born of God does not continue to sin; the One who was born of God keeps them _____, and the evil one _____ harm them. *(1 John 5:18)*

I Am Significant In Christ

You are the _____. But if the salt loses its saltiness, how can it be made salty again? It is no longer good for anything, except to be thrown out and trampled underfoot. You are the light of the world. A town built on a hill cannot be hidden. *(Matthew 5:13-14)*

I am the true vine, and my Father is the gardener. I am the vine; you are the _____. If you remain in me and I in you, you will _____; apart from me you can do nothing. *(John15:1, 5)*

You did not choose me, but I _____ you and
_____ you so that you might go and bear fruit—
fruit that will last—and so that whatever you ask in my name the
Father will give you. *(John 15:16)*

But you will receive power when the Holy Spirit comes on you; and
you will be my _____ in Jerusalem, and in all
Judea and Samaria, and to the ends of the earth. *(Acts 1:8)*

Don't you know that you yourselves are God's _____
and that God's Spirit dwells in your midst? *(1 Corinthians 3:16)*

Therefore, if anyone is in Christ, the new creation has come: The old
has gone, the new is here! All this is from God, who _____
us to himself through Christ and gave us the ministry of reconciliation:
that God was reconciling the world to himself in Christ, not counting
people's sins against them. And he has committed to us the message of
reconciliation. We are therefore Christ's _____,
as though God were making his appeal through us. We implore you on
Christ's behalf: Be reconciled to God. *(2 Corinthians 5:17-20)*

As God's _____ we urge you not to
receive God's grace in vain. *(2 Corinthians 6:1)*

And God _____ with Christ and
_____ in the heavenly realms in Christ Jesus. *(Ephesians 2:6)*

I keep asking that the God of our Lord Jesus Christ, the glorious Father, may give you the Spirit of wisdom and revelation, so that you may know him better. I pray that the eyes of your heart may be enlightened in order that you may know the _____
to which he has called you, the riches of his glorious inheritance in his holy people, and his _____ for us who believe. That power is the same as the _____ he exerted when he raised Christ from the dead and seated him at his right hand in the heavenly realms. *(Ephesians 1:17-18)*

For we are God's _____, created in Christ Jesus to do good works, which God _____ in advance for us to do. *(Ephesians 2:10)*

In him and through faith in him we may approach God with _____ and _____. *(Ephesians 3:12)*

I can do _____ through him who gives me strength. *(Philippians 4:13)*

But you are a _____ people, a royal_____, a holy nation, God's special _____, that you may declare the praises of him who called you out of darkness into his wonderful light. Once you were not a people, but now you are the_____; once you had not received mercy, but now you have received mercy. *(1 Peter 2:9-10)*

Did you discover your new identity in Christ? Can you truly perceive yourself as a child of God? Take a moment to review what you've just written. Then, take another moment and pray, asking God to help you receive the fullness of His revelation of your identity. Don't skip this step! As you partner with God in this moment, you have a precious opportunity to be transformed by the renewing of your mind!

Now, write your summary on the next page. This is your new bio!

Your Summary:
Who I Am In Christ

_____

_____

_____

_____

_____

_____

_____

_____

_____

_____

_____

_____

_____

_____

_____

_____

_____

_____

Prayer: A Lady's Identity

Dear Heavenly Father,

I know that You have given me a brand new identity that reflects Your likeness in me but I am not convinced that I am worthy of this image. Please Lord, impart Your revelation in me so that I know this new image is the transformation of Your image in me.

I ask You to forgive me of all my worldly ways and to cleanse me of all earthly identities, such as my reputation of physical, emotional, verbal and sexual abuse, my status of poverty and lack of prosperity, my angry personality; my drug and alcohol addictions, my low self-worth, my marital failure, the loneliness that surrounds me, the depression and anxiety, and my dysfunctional parenting habits. These "shame" identities have ruled my life long enough. I want the new me to come forth.

Remind me always of my new inheritance I have in You. I am so glad I don't have to wait till I get to heaven to know that I have been adopted into Your Kingdom forever. Help me to know and receive my significance as a "child of God," to understand how to walk in my new holiness, to be secure in my blamelessness, and to receive Your distinctiveness as my eternal character forever. Help me also to humble myself to this exclusive uniqueness of You within me always. I look forward to walking in my new identity. Thank You, Lord! Amen!

Group Discussion: Your Identity

1. Which question in the exercise did you most identify with? How does it describe you the most?

2. Did you conclude the truth of your value in Christ from reading the exercise questions? How valuable are you to Christ?

3. After completing the exercise, do you have a deeper sense of your identity in Christ? What light bulb went on for you?

4. What sentence in your summary most clearly shows your identity in Christ? Write it again here.

5. Which Scripture in the exercise did you struggle with most? Share your thoughts.

6. Does what you've written accurately reflect your innermost feelings about your identity? What are your true feelings about your God-given identity?

SECTION II

A LADY'S HEARTBEAT

"A fool vents all his feelings,
but a wise man [woman]
holds them back."
(Proverbs 29:11)

4

HER EMOTIONS

A LADY MANAGES HER EMOTIONS.
SHE DOES NOT LET HER FEELINGS LEAD HER LIFE.

Emotions, intellect, and will are the three components of a Lady's soul. A Lady has been designed by God to experience things through the part of the soul that "feels." She is hard-wired by God this way! The full range of emotions are a precious gift from God to help guide her. Through them, she can experience the love of Her Heavenly Father, be moved to tears by the beauty of a sunrise, and shout for joy at the sound of good news, or she can allow negativity to lead her into a pit of false beliefs, bitterness, and guilt. So, God charges her with the responsibility to be accountable for every thought, word, attitude, behavior, body language, and reaction. She is intended to be a victor in her responses, therefore her godly mission is to manage her emotions and not allow her emotions to manage her.

Unchecked negative emotions can produce over-dramatic displays of temper, prolonged depressive episodes, or harsh verbal outbursts, to name a few unpleasant effects. Living in this state long term often leads to broken relationships, unproductiveness, guilt, resentment, and increasing separation from God. Proverbs 14:17 cautions us with truth: *"A quick-tempered man acts foolishly, and a man of wicked intentions is hated."*

As a Lady, your victory is won when you do not react impulsively, rather assert your faith in God and respond in the likeness of Christ by the power of the Holy Spirit. Does this seem difficult to you, or even impossible? Just look for a moment at Who is on your team! With God as your coach, you cannot lose.

What Is God's Reason For Emotions?

Emotions are our first alert that something is happening that needs attention. Some emotions can be experienced without the need for immediate management, like joy, compassion, or even grief and anger at times. However, if our emotional reaction is excessive or prolonged and is not verified by our knowledge of God, we are likely to quickly find ourselves out of His will. God is abundantly present in our emotional life and uses our feelings to guide us toward His will, if only we are attuned to His voice. Let's take a closer look at some examples:

Fear
When fearfulness is present God may be alerting you to take caution. He wants you to be aware of upcoming hazards so you can address them with wisdom and truth. But, if you remain frozen in that state without peace and without taking action, you are allowing the spirit of fear to overtake you. 2 Timothy 1:7 says, *"For God has not given us a spirit of fear, but of power and of love and of a sound mind."* Soulishly, fear means that you are stagnant in fright, unable to believe that God will help you. It is a state of disconnectedness from Him. However, if you believe God's Word in Timothy, you know you have access to power from above, you are loved by God, and He will stabilize your mind with soundness so you won't have to let fear capture your life, having the upper hand.

Anger
Anger is a force that leads us to face our issues. This force drives us to address our problems. God wants us to move toward resolving our troubles as quickly as possible, because when anger is involved we can easily manipulate others, often without even knowing that we are being controlling. Ephesians 4:26-27 says, *"Be angry, and do not sin."* We have God's permission to be angry because there is usually reason for our anger. However, we are not permitted to sin against ourselves nor others with our angry reactions. Being angry was never meant for us to take advantage of someone or batter

them with our vengefulness. When you feel angry, this is a time to connect with God and cry out to Him about your hurt and pain. He wants you to grant Him the privilege of being your one and only loving God, to answer your needs, and to demonstrate His nature of mercy to you.

Guilt

Guilt says you have done something wrong and should prompt you to repent and ask forgiveness. Forgiveness ends guiltiness and repentance says you are willing to change your mind about cozying up with guilt as your best buddy. All that is required is a remorseful heart and a prayer to quickly reconnect you with God in righteousness. Numbers 5:6-7 makes it clear that, *"When a man or woman commits any sin...in unfaithfulness against the Lord, and that person is guilty, then he shall confess the sin which he has committed."* I have seen many people walk around with such feelings of guiltiness that their whole life becomes drudgery. They defend themselves rather than repent and it is a vicious cycle as they try to shake off guilt and can't. Guilt can only be removed through confession, repentance and the seeking of forgiveness. Once you have done this, God's assurance is that you have been redeemed by the blood of Jesus and you should not have to carry the weight of guiltiness any longer.

Shame

Shame expresses your humility and sorrow for certain circumstances. It is not a state of guilt as when you are convicted about your sin, but a state of embarrassment, humiliation and creates a setback in your perception of your value. God wants you to humbly seek truth at these times of shame and move beyond the reasons for humiliation. Psalms 71:1-2 says, *"Let me never be put to shame. Deliver me in your righteousness, and cause me to escape."* Feelings of shame capture our mind deceiving us that we could have changed some circumstance surrounding our shame. No, you are not capable of changing your parent's alcoholism or your uncle's nature of lewdness, however you can change your mind, believing you belong to Christ and you are the apple of your Lord's eye. Job knew exactly what his status was when saying, *"I put on righteousness, and it clothed me; My justice was like a robe and a turban"* (Job 29:14).

You are to become proactive and discard the feelings of shame and receive your righteousness in Christ.

Grief

Grieving is a normal and vitally necessary process of letting go and surrendering our feelings of loss to God. Through the grieving process we receive a new perspective, gradually yielding our desires, and facing reality at the hand of our loving Father. Ecclesiastes 7:3 says, *"By a sad countenance the heart is made better."* Grief says that we are low-spirited right now; we have lost something very valuable and important to us. Our tears wash away the sorrow and cleanse us from all of our hurts allowing God to console us. God asks us to entrust Him with the pleasure of comforting us and filling us with His way of relief at the time of these losses. Sadly, in today's world, few of us go through the full process of grieving. We choose to stay in anger and hurt, stuffing things down until we are drowning in depression, totally missing God's provision of mercy and healing. The recovery that comes with acceptance and forgiveness are too often never reached. Choosing to dwell in withdrawal with a frozen heart indicates a lack of surrender which can be hazardous to your well being. Continual feelings of loss and grief can become a full fledged spirit of grief—a stronghold that traps you in the bondage of self-pity until we repent of this menace.

Sadness

When we are sad God wants us to seek comfort in Him so we can work through our sorrows to come to joy again. 2 Corinthians 1:3-5 offers the wisdom, *"What a wonderful God we have—He is the Father of our Lord Jesus Christ, the source of every mercy, and the one who so wonderfully comforts and strengthens us in our hardships and trials. And why does he do this? So that when others are troubled, needing our sympathy and encouragement, we can pass on to them this same help and comfort God has given us"* (TLB). Feelings of sadness, bouts of pouting and controlling others with bad attitudes actually victimizes you by keeping you seeking pity in all the wrong places. Going to God for your pity and love is a sure path to finding and restoring your joy again.

Rejection

This emotion says that you or your ideas have not been received or accepted by another. In these moments, you need to remember that you are accepted and secure in Christ (see Chapter 3) so that you will be willing to forgive others quickly for their judgments against you. Ephesians 1:4-7 lets us know, *"He chose us in Him before the foundation of the world, that we should be holy and without blame before Him in love ….by which He made us accepted in the Beloved. In Him we have redemption through His blood, the forgiveness of sins, according to the riches of His grace."* Rejection is the major form of emotionalism that the devil uses to capture us. He convinces us that we are unwanted, exiled, banished from relationships, and viewed as worthless, damaged goods. Staying in the emotion of rejection is dangerous but recognizing that you are captured by your feelings and you want out, is a good place to be. You can ask God to forgive you for believing these lies and then repent that you no longer want to accept rejection as part of your identity.

Your emotions are meant to be used for your good. God cautions you in James 1:19-20 saying, *"So then, my beloved brethren, let every man be swift to hear, slow to speak, slow to wrath; for the wrath of man does not produce the righteousness of God."* Therefore, out-of-control feelings are not the best guide for making decisions. Improperly stewarded, emotions can be deceptive and lead you astray.

Negative or Positive Emotions—Which Will It Be?

We're talking about emotions, so let me paint an emotional picture for you. Imagine yourself in this situation:

> You hear some bad news; then you run to Fear and Worry and sit with them until Exaggeration, Deep Anxiety, Hopelessness and Dismay join you. Shortly thereafter Depression, Hurt and Anger come along to be with you too, leading you to argue back and forth with these deceptive characters all day long, into the next day, or even the next week.

In this scenario you have made this group of feelings your idol, by believing them and running to them repetitively as if they were your best friends. Whoa! Wrong group of friends! These friends have lied to you and made you believe that your issues cannot be resolved. Their voices have grown louder and become so familiar, they seem like the truth.

However, you could have run to God and chosen to sit with Faith, High Hope, Anticipation, Great Expectation, Joy, Comfort, Excitement, Contentment, Trust, and Enthusiasm. You could have invited Truth, Belief in God and Restoration to bring relief and a new resolution. You may not always have a ready smile and your answer may not always be around the corner, but these friends are the ones who will stay with you until God's promise is fulfilled.

Keys for Managing Your Emotions

Part of being a healthy Lady is to be able to experience a variety of feelings every day. Some of us want to hide our feelings and keep them secret while others want to express them in ways that get attention and cause disruption. Either extreme is not healthy or fruitful.

Scripture tells us to *"not let the sun set while we are still angry"* (Ephesians 4:26-27). There are two excellent reasons for this warning. First, the devil will take that anger and multiply it into a myriad of other emotions like bitterness, hatred, revenge, retaliation, resentment and mainly unforgiveness. Second, if we give ourselves to our negative or impulsive feelings, others will not be able to see Christ in us. Not only are you cheated out of your destiny, but so are those around you.

Psalm 4:4 says, *"Be angry, and do not sin. Meditate within your heart on your bed, and be still."* God gives you a clear picture of what He wants you to do when you are emotional. In a way, God is telling you to go to your room until you can calm down! In this passage He demonstrates how to dispel the extreme emotional responses of yelling, lashing out with your tongue, arguing and jostling with others for a position of control. God says to meditate *in your heart* while being *quiet and still*. I challenge you to do this the next time you want to lash out with anger.

With the right tools in your kit, all emotions can be brought into alignment with God's will and you can glorify Him with your victorious responses. A Lady has the finest quality tools at her disposal. Let's have a look inside the kit.

♥ **She Admits When She Needs Help.**
A Lady allows herself to speak about her struggles with her emotions to trusted others. She is brave and tells the truth to professional people who can help and guide her. She may join a support group or find a coach or mentor who can encourage and pray with her.

♥ **She Confesses She Has Been Deceived.**
If Satan can convince her to shift her attention from Christ to himself then he has won her loyalties, at least temporarily. But she is not to give allegiance to the devil! The Word says in James 4:7-10, *"Therefore submit to God. Resist the devil and he will flee from you. Draw near to God and He will draw near to you...Humble yourselves in the sight of the Lord, and He will lift you up."* She relies on this Scripture to guide her back to safety.

♥ **She Quickly Repents.**
Isaiah 55:7 says, *"Let the wicked forsake his way, and the unrighteous man his thoughts; Let him return to the Lord, and He will have mercy on him; and to our God, for He will abundantly pardon."* Repentance means changing direction from your own path toward destruction to God's prosperous direction for your life. A Lady does not hesitate to make a new decision to follow God in obedience to His Word.

♥ **She Surrenders Her Will.**
A Lady lays down all her reasons to be emotional, creating room in her to welcome and hold onto the truth of God's Word. 2 Corinthians 10:5 commands us to, *"...Cast down arguments and every high thing that exalts itself against the knowledge of God, bringing every thought into captivity to the obedience of Christ."* She gathers all the deceptive thoughts from the enemy and completely surrenders them to God, concluding that they are not useful or fruit producing. She knows these thoughts will destroy her if she uses her will to keep them as her truth.

♥ She Initiates Prayer.

Ephesians 5:15-17 *"So be careful how you act; these are difficult days. Don't be fools; be wise: make the most of every opportunity you have for doing good. Don't act thoughtlessly, but try to find out and do whatever the Lord wants you to"* (TLB). Reaching for God in prayer, before responding invites Him into your situation so He can help you to maintain a spiritual stance. God wants to be a partner with you, walking together in unity. However, when you walk away from Him you deny His covering for you and undermine His protection. Responding in a spiritual way is acclaiming Jesus as Lord in your life.

♥ She Takes Authority.

Luke 10:19 says, *"Behold, I give you the authority to trample on serpents and scorpions, and over all the power of the enemy, and nothing shall by any means hurt you."* God says you may use His name and the power it carries because you are His child. When you do, evil cannot remain. So, your declaration to the enemy is:

> "Satan, you cannot deceive me any longer with your lies; I command you to cease from hindering me and dominating my mind. I refuse to be caught up in this _____(name the emotion) any longer. In the mighty name of Jesus I pray."

You Have A Responsibility To God And Yourself

Becoming responsible for your emotional growth involves moving out of your comfort zone, taking risks, attempting change, and experiencing success *and failure* along the way—this is called progress. Progress leads to growth and growth to change. Change that results in you looking more like God is the process of sanctification. This process creates a productive Lady with emotional stability, able to give of herself to her church and community. The Holy Spirit dwelling in you creates a passion to seek after spiritual progress. It is up to you to respond to that gentle urging and not to quench it.

A great place to start is by working through conflict, not avoiding it, and learning to speak to others with love and kindness to resolve an issue. When you begin to believe new messages about yourself such as "Jesus loves you," you can let go of blaming others or yourself. Next, you will learn to move beyond blame and to reach resolution through prayer. Your responsibility includes making healthy choices to implement changes in your life such as seeking professional help, joining a support group, finding a coach or mentor, or visiting with your pastor.

Your greatest responsibility is to allow God to intervene in your life as a welcomed teacher, guide, and authority. The fullness of this is experienced when you respond to what the Holy Spirit is nudging you to do. The sooner you take your part by responding to Him in agreement (*response-ability*) the sooner you will reach your destiny of wholeness in Christ.

By now, you can see you're not in this alone. God will partner with you every step of the way, as long as you remember to include Him. Prayer is the ideal way to do just that. If you'll turn the page with me, I've given you five steps to surrendering your emotions in prayer. They are safe in God's care and so are you.

Steps for Surrendering Your Emotions in Prayer

Step One: *Admit* you are hurting.

Agreeing with God that you are hurting can then bring validation that your pain is real. This admission is to recognize that you are in need of God's help.

>*"I am hurting so badly right now with loneliness and forsakenness. I feel so cast out, deserted and abandoned..."*

Step Two: *Confess* your disappointment and loss.

God wants to hear what is on your mind. Tell Him what upsets you, how much your loss hurts, who did what to you and how it feels. He wants you to speak out every word, telling Him all about your broken heart.

>*"...they hurt me by _____ and I am experiencing loss of relationship, lack of comfort, rejection and the presence of this pain. I am broken and feeling lowly over this. I don't know what to do..."*

Step Three: *Express* your pain to God.

Cry, yell, toss and turn, shout and wail or silently weep with moaning whimpers in your pain! In intimate, private moments with God, many psalmists expressed their emotions in this way. Even Jesus, in his most troubled moment, cried out to *"Abba, Father!"* (Mark 14:36). God always hears when you cry.

>*"...I cry out to You in tears of despair Jesus, I am shattered in grief, sorrow and misery. HELP ME!"*

Step Four: *Surrender* your pain.

Surrendering means to give up the notion that it is up to you to fix your own pain. Full surrender means giving your pain over to God, trusting Him with it and willingly allowing Him to have every ounce of this horrible pain! You can accomplish this by deliberately turning your focus to Jesus in obedience to His word. While you're doing that, He is healing you.

>*"...I surrender my every will for retribution and recourse, turning this pain over to You to heal me and pay the price for it, Jesus. I let go of all this grief and sorrow, and I place it in Your hands..."*

Step Five: *Forgive* the person who hurt you.

Working toward complete forgiveness is a Lady's ultimate goal. This means you determine to totally pardon someone for their wrongdoing. It means granting clemency, pity, mercy and absolution. These may not be the words you most want to hear when you are in pain—you want justice, revenge, accountability and perhaps for someone to ache like you are aching—but a Lady follows God's commands and trusts in His promise that her forgiveness will bring freedom from her pain..

"...I forgive _____ of their sins against me right now and release them of expectations that they owe me anything for this offense in the name of Jesus. I refuse to walk in this pain, bitterness, and unforgiveness any longer. Please forgive me, Lord, for holding onto it for so long. Amen."

Prayer: A Lady's Emotions

Dear Precious Lord,

Thank You for giving me authority over my uncontrollable emotions. I was desperate to know what to do in these horrible moments of excessive pressure. I admit that I just went with the flow of outbursts and extreme demonstrations of despair. I was either silent in insecurity or bold in hostilities. I struggled with my inward self and what to do when under attack of the enemy. I realize that Satan was in charge of my soul more than I understood. Thank You, Lord, for prompting me to execute judgment and take authority over every assignment against me. I have been given prosperity, growth and maturity in Christ and I shall claim these words with power and might, all the days of my life.

Now I break the power of every evil order that has tried to trip me up and make me believe that my emotions should rule me. I remind you Satan that *no weapon formed against me shall prosper and every tongue which rises against me in judgment shall be condemned* (Isa 54:17). So, every stronghold of _____ (see list below) be GONE from my soul right now!

I ask You Lord to forgive me for believing the lies of the enemy and accepting emotionalism as my habit and friend. I repent of believing the wrong source. You are the Holy God and I will follow only You, not my soul's out-of-control emotions. Thank You for Your freedom over the opposition of emotions and relief from oppression and wrong authority. I shall continue to execute judgment over the enemy until he completely ceases from bothering me. In Jesus name I pray. Amen.

Emotional responses you might place in the blank above:

Unforgiveness	Fear	Insecurity	Anger	Pride
Stubbornness	Mistrust	Bitterness	Guilt	Hatred
Depression	Retaliation	Self-Hatred	Jealousy	Rebellion
Domination	Resentment	Self-Pity	Accusations	Shame
Hopelessness	Rejection	Despair	Strife	Control

Group Discussion: Your Emotions

1. Are you generally an emotional responder or more of a logical responder? Which way has worked best for you?

2. Have you struggled with being extremely emotional at times? How have you recovered when that has happened?

3. Have you tried to take authority over your emotional situations before? What technique did you use?

4. Have you experienced a time when emotionalism carried you away from God? Share one of your stories with the group.

5. Are you willing to use the process of admission, confession, expression, surrender, and forgiveness to reconcile your heart to God? Have you used this path before, only to take it all back?

6. Has emotionalism aided you in controlling and manipulating others to get your will? Is this the way that God wants you to conduct your life? What would be God's way?

*"Be sober-minded, in all things showing yourself to be
a pattern of good works;
in doctrine showing integrity, reverence, incorruptibility,
sound speech that cannot be condemned,
that one who is an opponent may be ashamed,
having nothing evil to say of you."
(Titus 2:6-8)*

HER INTEGRITY

A LADY MAKES AN EXCELLENT DECISION TO WALK IN INTEGRITY.
SHE DESIRES TO BE RIGHTEOUS AND HONEST IN ALL HER WAYS.

A Lady desires to please her Lord, with a pure heart full of integrity. She treats this decision as extremely important for the well being of her soul, and the righteous development of her good name. She wants her reputation to be without question, an open book for all to see. She acclaims the Word which says, *"He who walks with integrity walks securely, but he who perverts his ways will become known"* (Pro.10:9). In the light of God's matchless character she understands that she cannot be perfect, but through Jesus' sacrifice she was extended the benefit of God's grace. On the cross, His integrity became her integrity. Respectfully, she discovers through her faith in Christ, that she has the privilege of an excellent character before God—one that pleases Him as they walk together.

What Is Integrity?

Biblically, the word integrity means to be morally innocent, in godly perfection. Integrity is a characteristic of God's righteousness and is seen throughout the Bible as the "right path" or the "honest choice."[2] For you, integrity is the development of your blameless character, adhering to God's exemplary moral codes—choosing godly perfection every time you make a decision.

Integrity is not a high place of self-appointed righteousness. More accurately, it is a beautiful lowly place of meekness, submission and open surrender to God. 1 Peter 3:16 tells us to, *"Do what is right; then if men speak against you, calling you evil names, they will become ashamed of themselves for falsely accusing you when you have only done what is good."* (TLB) Your integrity is made up of an outward walk and an inward attitude to make a dogged determination to do what God says is right at all times.

As we explore the truth about integrity in the Bible, we find Colossians 3:10-11 telling us that we are: *"…living a brand new kind of life that is continually learning more and more of what is right, and trying constantly to be more and more like Christ who created this new life within you. In this new life one's nationality or race or education or social position is unimportant; such things mean nothing. Whether a person has Christ is what matters, and He is equally available to all"* (TLB).

When you make your decision to receive your new lifestyle of integrity, you will find yourself filtering your choices and responses through God's Word rather than resorting to old habits of thoughtless reactions or impulsive decisions. Scripture reminds us to, *"Keep a close watch on all you do and think. Stay true to what is right and God will bless you and use you to help others"* (1 Tim 4:16 TLB). Your daily commitment will be to make sure you are aligning yourself with God's commands and imitating His ways by choosing:

- ♥ To put away your self-centeredness by considering others around you above yourself.
- ♥ To take stock of your emotional responses and surrender your anger and fears to God.
- ♥ To leave your critical, judgmental attitude behind, and to purposefully make others feel accepted and comfortable in your presence.
- ♥ To begin to receive others as God's precious creations, made in His image, and looking at them through His eyes of mercy.

In the next few moments, take inventory of your present level of integrity, being honest with yourself to see where you can make some minor changes today. Consider writing in a journal or typing on your computer with a goal to keep working toward increasing your integrity. It will be well worth the effort and a very productive choice.

Guarding Against Temptation At All Times

Temptation is always waiting to pull us away from our integrity. It is rarely experienced as an obvious abduction, but usually as a sly deception, or a misleading ploy. Therefore, a Lady *must* be on guard at all times, by knowing and discerning God's complete truth. The devil has profoundly effective tactics and cunning enticements. Adam and Eve were our first examples of his manipulations. They faced deception and temptation and failed in integrity as Satan set them up to fall. The moment of their failure has sadly affected all of us from that day forward.

Satan starts deceiving us during our innocent years of childhood when our minds are not fully developed. He continues his deceitfulness in our adult years and sets out every day to have control over our minds. However, God's plan included a provision of hope for us against temptation. The Scripture reads like this, *"But this is the new agreement I will make with you…I will write my laws in their minds so that they will know what I want them to do without my even telling them and these laws will be in their hearts so that they will want to obey them, and I will be their God and they shall be my people"* (Heb 8:9-11 TLB). God gave us the ability to know His principle of integrity and to discern right from wrong. But, the choice is always ours. *"If you abide in My word, you are My disciples indeed. And you shall know the truth, and the truth shall make you free"* (Jn 8:31-32). The Word of God is our shield, protecting us against any temptation of the enemy.

Satan Tells Big Fat Lies

"The devil … was a murderer from the beginning and a hater of truth – there is not an iota of truth in him. When he lies, it is perfectly normal; for he is the father of liars" (Jn 8:44). Believe me, Satan will be your downfall in the area of integrity if you are not on guard at all times. He will continue to lie to you as long as you will entertain his deceptions. He has never told the truth and will never weary of his mission to persuade you that his lies are truth.

If you allow Satan's tactics to reign in your heart, your attitude, body language, behaviors, coping methods and your speech will sound just like him. You may use words of anger to manipulate others or you may put on a facial expression of spitefulness to frighten others away. You may even indulge in grudge-holding and spend hours thinking about how to get back at someone who hurt you. Years may pass where the subtle sin of unforgiveness has kept you from restoring relationship with a loved one without you fully realizing you chose this path so long ago. These choices become our identity when we believe Satan's lies rather than embrace the truth of God's Word. You were created far more beautifully than that!

It is a lie that you have to rebel, retaliate or snap in anger just to be heard or respected. Try using God's communication tools such as speaking with love from your heart, tempering your speech with gentleness, and offering olive branches of forgiveness. It pays huge dividends to give a response of love to any affront. (Rom 12:19).

If you have just realized you've been believing the lies of the enemy of your soul, keep in mind that God covers all sin through the finished work of the cross: *"And I will be merciful to them in their wrongdoings, and I will remember their sins no more"* (Heb 8:12). There is no lie that can stand up to your Savior's accomplishment. All you have to do is receive God's truth as your covering. What relief this message of redeeming hope brings to our minds when we have given into temptation!

Setting Clear Boundaries

Setting Boundaries is all about setting limits on yourself, not on others. It is NOT demanding that others stop doing something but it is establishing *what you will do* when and if they do something offensive against your ethics and boundary limits. Then you will have full control of yourself, being able to act according to your integrity and not their manipulation and control of you.

Establishing your boundaries ahead of time helps to prevent pressure and stress from capturing you at the time a clear mind is needed the most. Decision making under pressure can result in an impulsive choice you may regret. A godly, pre-determined decision assures you of having control and power when the pressure is on. Your choices are readily available and you can be confident in them.

For example: If a person asks you to go with them to an event you can simply respond with a pre-determined stall, "I will have to check with so-and-so to see what I might be obligated to that evening. Your boundary is to put some time between the invitation from others and your decision. You truly haven't decided if you want to go with this person. This boundary eliminates the pressure of answering immediately while under stress to respond. In this example you are placing time as your boundary so you have time to decide, pray and actually seek God for His response.

Another boundary you can set is one of distance between you and another. If a person is making a fuss at you, yelling and screaming, and asserting their temper, you have the privilege of asserting your response calmly by saying that you need to remove yourself from this situation until they can calmly speak to resolve this problem. The out-of-control person will then be distinguished as the one who needs help and not you. This puts the focus on them where it belongs. Scripture reminds us to *"...Behave carefully, taking life seriously. ... Let everything you do reflect your love of the truth and the fact that you are in dead earnest about it. Your conversation should be so sensible and logical that anyone who wants to argue will be ashamed of himself because there won't be anything to criticize in anything you say"* (Titus 2:6-8 TLB). Setting your limits in place before something develops is a life-saving endeavor for your spiritual health and well being.

Vigilant Prayer for Sustained Integrity

Asking God for help in maintaining your integrity is a great act of love toward yourself. His response will always be to help you. Psalm 46:1 verifies this by saying, *"God is our refuge and strength, a very present help in trouble."*

Imagine if your child needed help but she did not ask you for it. How would you feel if you could not help her simply because she did not ask? It is a pretty powerless position to be in. You possessed all the tools necessary to intervene, except the invitation did not come forth. Would you feel pretty sad or left-out? I would!

A lady related to me that her daughter was raped at the age of ten but when she finally decided to tell her mother, she was thirty-something in years. The mother was devastated and wondering why she did not tell her about this horrible incident. The mother took a long time to forgive herself for not knowing about this and not being able to help her child at the time. Also, she had to forgive the daughter for waiting so long to share her burden. This same thing happens with God. When we fail to talk to Him about our situations and ask for His help, He may not move on our behalf. Our Heavenly Father is a gentleman and often waits for us to bring our needs to Him. John 16:24 clarifies to us, *"Until now you have asked nothing in My name. Ask, and you will receive, that your joy may be full."* Therefore, we just need to pray with a heart of love toward Him as our provider, comforter, and Savior. When we do, we are assured, as in 1 John 5:15, which says, *"And if we know that He hears us, whatever we ask, we know that we have the petitions that we have asked of Him."* Keeping this perspective of John in mind, we must conclude that all God wants is an invitation (to be asked) to impart help to us in times of need.

Why don't we pray and ask? Some reasons are because we don't understand the sacrifice of Christ or we don't believe He answers our prayers, or we don't see God as having an interest in us or we don't think God is big enough to handle our trials. Some of us don't feel worthy to ask and then again, others ask for the wrong things and reasons. His Word reminds us: *"So I say to you, ask, and it will be given to you; seek, and you will find; knock, and it will be opened to you. For everyone who asks receives, and he who seeks finds, and to him who knocks it will be opened. If a son asks for bread from any father among you, will he give him a stone? Or if he asks for a fish, will he give him a serpent instead of a fish? Or if he asks for an egg, will he offer him a scorpion?"* (Luke 11:9-12).

God is not a closed-ear God! He wants to hear your every need and answer your every appeal. If His Word tells us what to do then take up the custom of doing it! God means every Word He says! Therefore, ask and you will receive. "I *say to you, whatever things you ask when you pray, believe that you receive them, and you will have them"* (Mark 11:24).

Learning and Growing From Our Failures

We are to mature in all things as we grow in Christ. After going through a trial, ask yourself, "What have I learned?" Then ask God to reveal to you what this experience has taught you. Through experiences you can gain perspective from your moral failures, your emotional disasters and even your physical traumas and trials. You can learn to put your failures behind you and walk in integrity. Trials will come to everyone walking this earth. Matthew 5:45 affirms this truth: *"He makes*

His sun rise on the evil and on the good, and sends rain on the just and on the unjust." However, what counts when going through your rainstorms is how you respond to getting wet. When we submit ourselves to God's correction and training, we are assured that we will grow into Ladies of integrity. Our walk and our talk will match up with His, our lives will be a testimony to His greatness, and He will be glorified in our every interaction.

Prayer: A Lady's Integrity

Dear Lord,

Please forgive me for not reaching for your standard of integrity. I have fallen short of your glory and have not been honest with myself or You in areas of moral maturity and right choices. You have given me all that I need to make godly decisions, but I have ignored Your truth.

Help me to identify my shortcomings and be willing to release my own standard of integrity to take on Yours. I desire to align my walk with You Lord, bringing my faith, mind, will, and emotions to embrace your Word. Guide me through the process of setting good boundaries with myself, knowing that I can undermine my own integrity at times. Show me where I have been believing the lies of Satan over Your magnificent truth.

Lord, I desire to change my life to meet Your greatness in integrity. Help me to accomplish this endeavor. Amen.

Group Discussion: Your Integrity

1. What does integrity mean to you? How have you been applying it to your life?

2. On a scale of 1 to 10, with 10 being highest, where is your level of integrity? Why is it where it is? Where would you like it to be?

3. Have you chosen a method of expressing your boundary line when faced with pressure and stress of last minute decision making? Are you more comfortable responding in the moment, or is a predetermined choice better for you?

4. Do you struggle with the temptation to leave your integrity behind, taking up attitudes and behaviors unbecoming of a godly Lady? What are God's solutions to your dilemma?

5. Have you asked God to help you establish your integrity? Why? Why not?

6. Is honesty from your heart something that you have evaded? If so, why have you evaded it?

"Let not mercy and truth forsake you;
Bind them around your neck,
Write them on the tablet of your heart,
And so find favor and high esteem
In the sight of God and man."
(Proverbs 3:3-4)

6

HER ESTEEM

A LADY DOES NOT SECRETLY DESPISE HERSELF.
SHE BUILDS SELF-ESTEEM ON HER ACCEPTANCE AND GRACE IN CHRIST.

Did you ever see a Lady oozing with esteem? She emits self-approval, self-acceptance and self-confidence with grace and refinement that tells others that she has canceled the judgment of condemnation and indebtedness against herself. She stands tall with confidence and poise. Her self-esteem does not vacillate—it stays steady. How did she become so refined and centered on Christ? The answer is simple and perfect: through God's grace. Since grace is available to every Lady who will receive it, so is self-esteem. Let's talk about it, shall we?

God's Message of Grace

Grace is the favor and kindness shown to you without considering your efforts or achievements. Grace does not take into consideration whether or not you deserve this favor. God distributes grace to us according to His pleasure and goodwill. His grace was given at the cross through Christ and therefore is related to His love, mercy, and compassion for you personally. This favor was not earned by you—but was given to you through God's precious desire to simply give you what He knows you need to thrive. Can you picture the parents of a two year old choosing to give their child food, shelter, clean clothes, and love? The parents choose to give because they *want to give*, not because the child has earned or deserved their portion. This picture is the same view of God's grace with us.

God's message of grace is in Ephesians 1:7-8 which says, *"So overflowing is his kindness toward us that He took away all our sins through the blood of his Son… and He has showered down upon us the richness of his grace— for how well He understands us and knows what is best for us at all times"* (TLB). God understands you and knows that love is the only answer to your every need. As He loves you through His extension of grace, you are to love yourself and then reflect this love to others. Often, the hardest part of this cycle is to extend love to yourself. This is where developing your self-esteem must become a personal pursuit on your behalf including surrendering the grievances you have against yourself. When you can accept and love yourself by seeing yourself through God's eyes, your self-esteem will follow suit. One clue that you're making good progress is that it becomes your heart's desire to extend this love, in turn, to others. Ask yourself, "Do I really love myself and accept everything about myself including my shortcomings and weaknesses?" When you can honestly say from your heart, "Yes," you will know that you are developing and embracing the grace of self-esteem.

What is Self-Esteem?

Your self-esteem is the foundation for your confidence and the assurance of who you believe you really are. It consists of an attitude and perception about yourself and the hope of who you think you can become. Esteeming yourself means:

- ♥ To *approve* of yourself, including all your imperfection.
- ♥ To *respect* yourself, treating yourself with value and worth.
- ♥ To *appreciate* yourself and how God magnificently created you.
- ♥ To *love* yourself with your God given talents and spiritual gifts.
- ♥ To *like* yourself by having grace upon yourself as Christ does.

Jesus considered all of your positive aspects like: your humanness, your accomplishments, your maturity, your appearance, your talents, and your gifts as well as your negative aspects like your failures, mistakes, and sins as He went to the cross. He agreed that it was worth it to Him and He willingly wanted to pay the price for your life. He loved you so much that He took your sins on himself so that they would not be an obstacle between God and you. Therefore, God can commune with you, abide in you, and accomplish His purposes through you.

He wants you to regard yourself with this same kind of favor called *grace* so that self-rejection (personal dislike for who you are) will not be in the way of your relationship with Him. Self-acceptance is the key to having well-developed self-esteem. If Jesus accepted you then you ought to accept yourself. Ephesians 1:6 says, *"He made us accepted in the Beloved."* "He made us" means that He took care of everything that interfered with you sharing your life with Him therefore, you are acceptable to God.

The Path To a Ladies Esteem

There are a number of significant things you can do to build and mold your self-esteem so that you can live your life with a positive and accurate assessment of your personal worth. The staircase that leads to your improved self-esteem looks like this:

1. **Accept yourself just as you are**.
   If you accept yourself as the beautiful human being you were created to be, you align yourself with the truth of Christ. What do you personally disapprove of or despise in yourselves? What's at the top of your list? Is it your hair, your height, your emotions, your facial features, or perhaps just your life in general? Are you secretly ashamed of what you look like or who you really are inside? Are you professing, "I hate myself. I hate my life?" Have you ever thought that you wished you were dead or that the world would be better off without you? Be honest with yourself.

   Despising yourself means that you are not satisfied with how God created you. Continual self-hatred creates shame then shame leads to self-rejection and self-rejection leads to death of your character. This in turn will lead to death of your Spirit. When you have totally rejected yourself, you will have fallen into the hands of the devil agreeing with his voice over God's.

Ladies, please know that God loves you just the way you are. You are to love yourself and approve of every little thing about yourself. You, as God's Lady, were created in the image of Him. He formed you in your mother's womb just the way He wanted you to look and be (Psalm 139). He enjoys gazing upon your personal beauty every time He communes with you. Even if you have altered your features with plastic surgery, hair coloring or gobs of make-up your outside image is all that has changed. There is lots of grace and mercy in beautifying yourself, however the reference here is to the over-indulgence and extreme use of reconstructing your features because YOU inwardly hate yourself. We don't need a face lift Ladies, we need a *HEART LIFT!*

2. **Be truthful with yourself.**

Proverbs 3:3-4 says, *"Let not mercy and truth forsake you; bind them around your neck, write them on the tablet of your heart, and so find favor and high esteem in the sight of God and man."* True honesty from your heart is the type of inner beauty that identifies your imperfections yet is able to accept every one of them as being a part of a beautiful you. Your self-acceptance without self-judgment is the mark of healing your esteem. What is it you need to tell the truth about? Being honest about your integrity, humility, pride, submission, regrets, doubts, fears, anger, unbelief, and envies is part of coming out of denial and into truthfulness. Do some of the things on that list sound familiar? Romans 12:3 tells us to, *"Be honest in your estimate of yourselves, measuring your value by how much faith God has given you"* (TLB). This type of faith equates to loving yourself as God loves you.

Through this measure of faith you can display your confidence of laughing without hesitation, being creative and inspired without shame, being challenged but not fearful, or stretched without panic. This type of faith is the freedom to let your girly side show with all of its ruffles, tears and joys. With this faith you are able to express your interests, passions and pleasures without embarrassment or apologies. Faith is being able to have a patient attitude granting yourself permission to just be YOU. It brings a comfortableness that outweighs self-condemnation. A Lady can look in the mirror with truthfulness and claim she has shortcomings yet knows her righteousness in Christ as her measure of esteem.

3. **Give up perfectionism.**
   The world convinces us that we need to look perfect, act perfect and perform with perfection. We are prodded by the TV, movies and media that we should all look a certain way, appearing and acting faultless and flawless. We are convinced to secretly covet someone else's body features and appearance and seduced into believing that we should look exactly like the movie stars. Did you know that it is impossible to look, act or be perfect? There has only ever been one perfect person and His name is Jesus. By following Him, He graciously makes us perfect in God's sight.

4. **Be proud of the unique and special person God created you to be.**
   Treat yourself with respect and value when regarding or talking to or about yourself. Believe that you are whom God desires you to be and tell yourself to operate on the truth that your opinions, beliefs, and needs are valid in God's eyes. Tell yourself, "God loves me no matter what I do wrong." "He has made me special so I am special to Him." "I am the King's kid." "Jesus loves me this I know." "Greater is He that is in me than he who is in the world." Expounding upon scriptures can build your esteem quickly. Don't forget that you are beautifully and wonderfully made into HIS likeness and made prefect in His presence.

5. **Confess, repent and forgive yourself.**
   Mistakes, flaws and failures are an everyday part of our lives as human beings, so accept your humanness without shame or embarrassment. Practice forgiving yourself, and place all of your failures in God's hands. Get in touch with your feelings by learning to recognize them and how you have believed that they were your source of redemption instead of Jesus. When you feel guilty or depressed, ask yourself, "Where do these

emotions come from?" Your emotions may have come from some painful experience in childhood, or from adolescent experiences of inadequacy, or from a self-defeating message that plays and replays in the back of your mind. When you fall short of righteousness and fall into sin simply confess your trespasses, ask for forgiveness and repent of believing those lies again. Choose confession, forgiveness and repentance as your way of bringing closure to your unrighteousness forever.

6. **Think, speak, and act positively.**
   Replace your negative self-talk with positive self-talk. What is self-talk? It is the *repeated messages you tell yourself* whether unconsciously or consciously. Some of these messages are negative: "I can't do it," "I always foul up," "I'm so dumb," "I hate myself." As you learn to replace these assumptions with positive statements from scripture, your self-esteem will grow. Begin by replacing negative messages with positive messages that say, "I can do all things through Christ who strengthens me...." and "I will because God is on my side...." "I am accepted in the Beloved..." "I am bought by the blood of Jesus..." These are promises from your Heavenly Father, who loves you dearly. He made them for you to stand on, like a high, flat rock in the middle of an ocean.

7. **Learn to accept praise from others.**
   Ladies with low self-esteem tend to disbelieve righteous compliments or make a self-depreciating remark when praised. Learn to examine what others might say to you instead of discounting their comments and advice. You might find that they are giving you a message from God or presenting a truth that you did not formerly understand or know about yourself. Often, other people recognize qualities in us that we can't see. As you learn to see yourselves as others see you, you will begin to grow and find healing in your self-esteem.

8. **Do not envy others or what they have.**
   Avoid the trap of the enemy called "envy." We often reject ourselves when we realize what others have or possess,

wondering why we don't have those same delights, gifts, talents, or joys. This mindset beats down your self-esteem very quickly. Don't ask of the Lord, "Why do they have this or that…" but simply ask Him for what you want. John 16:24 says, *"Until now you have asked nothing in My name. Ask, and you will receive, that your joy may be full."*

What someone else has is theirs—it was given to them by God. Your Heavenly Father has plenty of promises for you to have your portion too. He knows exactly what you need to fulfill the purpose for which you were created and He will provide it at just the right time. So, empty your hands and surrender your envy for what others have and He will deliver *your* destiny in His time. Your goal is to become satisfied and thankful with what God has given you and with the person He has made you to be.

A true Lady realizes that she is not the "fairest" of them all—she knows her Lord as the only true perfect One. She knows that if she fails that there is grace for her flaws, forgiveness for her heart and mercy to be received in abundance. Have you ever heard it said that "beauty is only skin deep?" This is only true in a culture that defines beauty by outward appearance. Genuine beauty comes from the heart and the most beautiful among us are those hearts that beat for God. When He made the provision of redemption available to you through Jesus' blood, He gave you abundant grace, expecting you to live by your heart and not by your efforts to be perfect in His or anyone else's eyes. He created you to be you and He loves you that way!

You are given the choice of inner beauty with every decision that you make. God allows you to have your free will. So, whenever your self-esteem is challenged, the answer is always to surrender your will to Christ. Yes, it is that simple. Surrendering your will and accepting *God's will* establishes that your heart is with Him. Surrendering in this way is a life-long process—an ongoing shrinking of the flesh and growing of the Spirit. By now, you should be able to see that liking yourself is really the second priority you have as a Christian—the first priority is to love God. Jesus speaks in Matthew 22:37-39 saying, *"… you shall love the Lord your God with all your heart, with all your soul, and with all your mind. This is the first and great commandment. And the second is like it: you shall love your neighbor as yourself."* The progression of *first,* loving Him, then *second,* accepting and loving yourself because of what He has done for you, and then *third* ministering that love to others is the necessary order for any of the steps to be accomplished fully.

The hidden and secret ways of self-hatred will vanish when you realize the love of Christ and the price He paid for your life. Your low self-esteem and your inner attitude of disrespect or rejection toward yourself will fade away. Then the acceptance of your "identity in Christ" will be full and complete and your behaviors, responses, and reactions toward yourself will begin to align with God's grace in you. Your low self-esteem will be exchanged for Christ-like esteem in loving and valuing yourself as God does.

Prayer: A Lady's Esteem

Dear Lord, Jesus,

Forgive me for all the times that I made poor choices to despise myself, disliking who I was, being ashamed at how I looked and indulging in negative ways against myself. I, so often, told myself that I was dumb and stupid, ugly and shameful. This was a mistake Lord, and I repent of those worldly deceptions. Release me and cleanse me of all unrighteousness. I choose this day to align my will with Your will, Lord, to believe that *"...I am fearfully and wonderfully made; marvelous are Your works,"* (Psa 139:14) and *"How precious also are Your thoughts to me, O God! How great is the sum of them! If I should count them, they would be more in number than the sand..."* (Psalms 139:17-18)

Thank You for creating me as Your beautiful creation. You have redeemed me from self-hatred and given me a wonderful worth in You. You justified me, acquitted me and You have set my reputation precisely in righteousness with You. Your Word presents me with new esteem. Just knowing that I am Your child and You are my Father is comforting to my soul. Guide me from here and help me to know righteousness in Christ from this point forward. I thank You for Your love for me and my new esteem in You. Amen.

Group Discussion: Your Esteem

1. Are you struggling with developing your self-esteem? Why?

2. At what point did you discover that you must build your self-esteem with God's help. How low did you allow yourself to go before taking charge of your esteem?

3. Have you falsely transferred your responsibility of building your self-esteem in Christ to others around you. Have you waited for their opinion of you to boost your esteem? Why did you transfer your responsibility to them? Do they know your heart?

4. What do you do to respect yourself? Emotionally? Physically? Socially? Spiritually?

5. How would you like God to help you with your esteem? Is your heart ready to allow God to reveal Himself to you?

6. Read Psalms 139 out loud. Do you recognize how marvelous you are to God? Share your wonderment of how he created you in His image.

SECTION III

*A LADY'S
SPIRIT*

"The character of even a child can be known
by the way he acts
whether what he does is pure and right."
(Proverbs 20:11 TLB)

HER CHARACTER

A LADY GLEAMS BRIGHTLY IN HER CHRISTIAN CHARACTER.
SHE LOOKS TO GOD AS HER EXAMPLE OF RIGHTEOUSNESS.

A Lady embraces her Lord's holy character as the reflection of Jesus in her heart. Discipline, self-control, peace, gentleness, assurance, and respect, are just some of the beautiful new character traits that reflect through her. She looks so pretty wearing these glowing traits, which she acquired by humbling herself before her Lord. She knows what she allows to rule her heart forms her character. She reveres Jesus as her Lord and seeks after Him all of her days. In turn, step-by-step, He changes her to match His own loving character, adding, *"... virtue, and to virtue knowledge, to knowledge self-control, to self-control perseverance, to perseverance godliness, to godliness brotherly kindness, and to brotherly kindness love"* (2 Peter 1:5-9). She becomes aware of her new heart and agrees with God that her "old nature" must go. She treasures His priceless character at work in her, and thrills at the notion that all of His traits can be hers if she chooses to love Him with all of her heart.

What Is A Christ-like Character?

The Bible describes a godly character as your distinctive qualities that reflect the image of Christ within you, including your behavior choices, conduct, attitudes, thoughts, words and deeds. As a Christian, you are called to permit the gospel of Jesus to mold and renew your mind. In doing so, a transforming regeneration of your character occurs. God gives you the opportunity and the power to take on His unique character and to cast away everything that does not glorify Him. The Apostle Paul describes this process as putting on the holy character or the "new man" and taking off the corrupt character or the "old man."

Every Christian Lady is charged by God to build a new godly-character within her heart and mind as 2 Peter 3:18 tells us, *"But grow in the grace and knowledge of our Lord and Savior Jesus Christ."* Building such character takes time (in fact, it takes a lifetime) and a deliberate choice to apply Scriptural principles to your everyday life. It also includes humbling yourself before Him in prayer, praise, worship, and thankfulness, and *"bringing every thought into captivity to the obedience of Christ"* (2 Cor 10:5).

The Bible presents a spiritual path and beckons you to choose it, then reveals how to conduct your life accordingly. If you choose to move forward on this path, these spiritual choices will produce your good character—called "good fruit," and result in conformity with the will of God. Like an expert silversmith, God polishes and purifies you until He sees His face reflected in you. If, however, you turn away from this path and choose another, then you will go around this "character-building" mountain again and again. Until your heart gives in to accept the truth that Jesus Christ is Lord, you cannot be completely at peace because you aren't operating the way you were created to.

In 1 Corinthians 2:15-16 the Bible shares with us, *"the spiritual man has insight into everything, and that bothers and baffles the man of the world, who can't understand Him at all... But, strange as it seems, we Christians actually do have within us a portion of the very thoughts and mind of Christ"* (TLB). This "portion" is within you because of who your heavenly Father is. It would be a shame to leave that potential untapped or, worse, to actively work against it for your entire life. Look down the path with the bright lights on the stepping stones, and take His hand as you step surely on the first one.

Character Building

Here are eight key things you can do to sharpen your character into the image of God. This certainly isn't all you need to consider, but if you commit to these suggestions and make them a priority and a habit, you'll begin to look a lot like your Lord—to yourself and to others.

1. **Make Knowing God Your Top Priority.**

    This is not always easy to do especially when you are over-taxed for time with your career, keeping a home, raising children, helping with church duties, communing with friends, and serving in the community. Many things require your time, however intimacy with God needs to be a lifetime priority. You will want to get to know Him personally and not just know *about* Him. Titus 1:16 explains that some of us have only gone through the motions of knowing God but do not truly know Him intimately as a real person, *"They profess to know God, but in works they deny Him..."*

    2 Peter 1:2-3 poses this question to the Christian: *"Do you want more and more of God's kindness and peace? Then learn to know him better and better. For as you know him better, he will give you, through his great power, everything you need for living a truly good life"* (TLB). Getting to know God is a life-long journey. So don't ever stop seeking to experience the heart of intimacy with Him.

2. **Clean-Up Your Speech.**

    Cleaning-up your speech is usually one of the first transitions that takes place in a new Christian's life. Often, a new believer begins to acknowledge that their words need to be pure and holy, tempered and uncorrupt. *"Let your speech always be with grace, seasoned with salt, that you may know how you ought to answer each one"* (Col 4:6). Express yourself without the sensationalism and allure of foul language. Jesus did not curse or use polluted or profane language to make His point; you should not make it part of your character image either.

3. **Accept Responsibility For Your Mind.**

    One area in which you will want to be honest with yourself is: Who are you spending your time with in your mind? Are you communing with God all day or are you listening to the devil, agreeing with the downward spiral of arguments and lies that he offers. If anger, rage, resentments, depression, regrets, unforgiveness, bitterness, and rejection are your mind's best friends then you have not taken responsibility to know the truth of God's love. Precisely knowing that your mind is to be fixed on Christ can keep you out of the pits and usher you into the reality of heaven. The Apostle Paul calls you to take responsibility for managing your mind and thoughts, "*casting down all arguments and every high thing that exalts itself against the knowledge of God, bringing every thought into captivity to the obedience of Christ*" (2 Cor 10:5). When you allow your thoughts to dwell on anything other than God and His promises, there is always a possibility that you will be jostling back and forth with the devil. It may sound something like this in your mind:

"NO!" you say. "I don't need to get into this with John. It is not his fault."

"YES!" insists the devil, "It is John's fault, you know it is."

"NO," you say. "I just need to be calm with my eyes on Jesus."

"YES," persists the devil. "John did this to hurt you."

"No...he didn't... well maybe...he *was* kind of disrespectful to me," you concede.

"YES! You know what you should do to get even with this fellow," roars the devil.

"Well...Yeah," you say in your anger and indignation, "Maybe I should disrespect him like he did me."

"YES," acclaims the devil. "You are justified in what you want to do to him. He deserves it."

"YES, you are right," you say. "He is totally to blame for all of this!"

"YES, he never liked you anyway. Now go pounce all over him and give him a piece of your mind," says the devil.

At this point, the enemy has captured your mind, convincing you to say "Yes," to his schemes. You have given in to the deception and surrendered the victory to him for this round. He wants to keep your mind distracted with arguments, lies, blame, pride, jealousies, fears, and judgments. If you allow it, there's little or no room for the things of God.

You know you need to keep your whole mind on Christ, but how? The answer is to repent (turn away) from following the enemy's will and meditate on Scripture as your source of life and truth. God's encouragement to you at these times of battle is, *"Fix your thoughts on what is true and good and right. Think about things that are pure and lovely, and dwell on the fine, good things in others. Think about all you can praise God for and be glad about."* (Phil 4:8 TLB).

4. **Be Purposed In Your Calling.**
God created you with His purpose in mind. He desires for you to be purposeful in exampling Him to everyone you meet. He provides you with specific gifts, certain talents, leadership abilities, and a particular direction for your life to flow. Do not just drift through life taking what may come your way. You must aim for God's will, establishing spiritual goals and working purposefully to reach them. Be determined to persevere and be obedient to His gentle nudging. Check yourself for stubbornness and unwillingness, never forgetting that your ultimate goal is to spend eternity with Him and not separated from Him. In Acts 26:16-18 we see God addressing Saul (who became Paul the Apostle) about his call to work for Him, *"Now stand up! For I have appeared to you to appoint you as my servant and my witness. You are to tell the world about this experience and about the many other occasions when I shall appear to you."* What a clear purpose Paul was called to!

A Lady's commission from God is very similar to Paul's. Matthew 28:19-20 tells you to, *"Go therefore and make disciples of all the nations, baptizing them in the name of the Father and of the Son and of the Holy Spirit, teaching them to observe all things that I have commanded you; and lo, I am with you always, even to the end of the age."* This does not always mean placing your feet on foreign soil in order to accomplish this command but it does mean that you were called according to God's will. Many of you reading this now are meant to discover your Kingdom purpose and to use your special talents and gifts to produce God's will right where you are today and every day hereafter. *"So I say to you, ask, and it will be given to you; seek, and you will find; knock, and it will be opened to you. For everyone who asks receives, and he who seeks finds, and to him who knocks it will be opened"* (Lk 11:9-11). Whether you are on familiar ground or far from home, you are to be about your Father's business.

5. **Form Spiritual Habits.**
   A habit is a custom or routine that you practice again and again without even thinking about doing it. It is done automatically. We are told in 1 Timothy 4:7-9 to keep spiritually fit such as *"Don't waste time arguing over foolish ideas and silly myths and legends. Spend your time and energy in the exercise of keeping spiritually fit. Bodily exercise is all right, but spiritual exercise is much more important and is a tonic for all you do. So exercise yourself spiritually, and practice being a better Christian because that will help you not only now in this life, but in the next life too"* (TBL). God requests us to become proactive in spiritual practices like reading the Bible, meditating on His Word, praying, forgiving others, surrendering your heart to God, preaching the gospel to the unsaved and so on. To succeed, you'll want to make forming spiritual habits part of your everyday routine.

6. **Conduct Your Behavior According to God's Word.**
   A good rule when it comes to managing your behavior is: "Don't do anything you would not want to be doing when Jesus comes back." If you haven't already developed a policy of righteous conduct in your daily life, cultivate and implement a policy of thankfulness and patience to fill up the space that will be freed up when you cut off vengefulness and irritability at their root. 1 Thessalonians 5:14-22 expounds a little further by saying, *"Dear brothers...comfort those who are frightened, take tender care of those who are weak, and be patient with everyone. See that no one pays back evil for evil, but always try to do good to each other and to everyone else. Always be joyful. Always keep on praying. No matter what happens, always be thankful, for this is God's will for you who belong to Christ Jesus. Do not smother the Holy Spirit. Do not scoff at those who prophesy, but test everything that is said to be sure it is true, and if it is, then accept it. Keep away from every kind of evil"* (TLB). Always take your behavior examples from the Word of God.

7. **Discipline Yourself.**
   Discipline is practicing control and restraints in methods of character modeling and acceptable codes of conduct. It also means to obey the given rules and follow certain authority

figures who have leadership over you. When we think of discipline, often impressions of punishment and chastisement come to mind. But God does not want to punish us—He would prefer to persuade our will to be in agreement with His will through His display of love for us.

From a biblical perspective, discipline means to take command over your "flesh" denying your worldly interests for the sake of your walk with God. Denying your flesh means rejecting or disowning things of the world that stand in the way of your relationship with God. It calls upon you to say "no" to evil habits, the influences of the wrong friends, addictions (drugs, alcohol and codependency), using profanity, and everything like this. Submitting to and practicing discipline helps your mind grow from an undeveloped, juvenile one into the mature mind of Christ. Jesus reminds us in Matthew 16:24, *"If anyone wants to be a follower of mine, let him deny himself and take up his cross and follow me."*

8. **Choose To Be A Lady In Christ.**
   A Christian Lady is one who wears the name of the Lord Jesus in her heart. It shows that she belongs to Jesus and that she is living in harmony with God's will. Claiming to be a Christian but not being willing to conform your life (your thoughts, actions, decisions, and will) to His principles is insincere, ineffective faith. 2 John 9 says, *"For if you wander beyond the teaching of Christ, you will leave God behind; while if you are loyal to Christ's teachings, you will have God too. Then you will have both the Father and the Son"* (TLB). Your honesty about the condition of your heart toward God is one of the main ingredients needed to partner with Him on your life's journey.

To help establish crystal clarity on what a conformed life looks like, I've put together the chart on the next two pages, which contrasts worldly characters with godly characters. Mark the terms that jump out at you on both lists to help you understand your strengths and struggles. These are points of prayer for you.

CHARACTERISTICS OF THE WORLDLY

Abominable	Hypocritical
Alienated from God	Loathsome
Blasphemous	Lover of pleasure
Blinded, Ignorant of God	Lying
Boastful	Mischievous
Conspiring against saints	Murderous
Corrupt	Perverse
Covetous	Prayerless
Deceitful	Proud
Delighting in the iniquity of others	Persecuting others
Defiant	Rebellious
Despising saints	Reprobate
Destructive	Selfish
Disobedient,	Sensual
Enticing to Evil	Sold out for Sin
Envious	Stiff-Hearted
Evildoer	Stiff-Necked
Fearful	Unclean
Hard-hearted	Unjust
Foolish	Unmerciful
Forgetting God	Ungodly Fierce
Fraudulent	Unholy
Glorying in their shame	Unthankful
Hating the light	Unprofitable,
High-minded	Unruly
Hostile to God	Unwise

CHARACTERISTICS OF THE GODLY

Attentive to Christ's voice	Hunger for righteousness
Blameless	Joyful
Bold in Christ's Spirit	Just and true
Committed	Kindly
Compassionate	Led by the Spirit
Contrite in heart	Liberal in Christ's character
Dependable	Loathing the flesh
Devout	Lovingly
Discerning	Loving others and self
Faithful	Lowly in Spirit
Fearing God in reverence	Loyal
Following in obedience	Meek
Forgiving	Merciful
Forsaking sins	Patient
Graceful	Peace-Loving
Gentle	Prudent
Godly in character	Submissive
Guileless	Truthful
Harmless in deeds	Trustworthy
Holy and pure	Understanding
Humble	Wise in Christ

Did you see the contrast between the two lists? On which list did you discover more of your character? Honestly evaluate where you are presently so you can adjust your aim to hit the goal of righteousness. Don't feel upset if it looks like you have work to do. I'm sure you're not alone at that party! Instead, celebrate the good news that this is a new day and you are taking a step toward victory with unreserved assistance from God.

The Fruit of Christ's Character

Galatians 5:22-23 tells us that you will produce a crop of spiritual fruit from obedience to Christ's teachings, *"But the fruit of the Spirit is love, joy, peace, longsuffering, kindness, goodness, faithfulness, gentleness, and self-control."* Your old worldly fruits of hatred, discontentment, anxiousness, impatience, rudeness, dishonesty, unfaithfulness, harshness, and lack of control will gradually pass away, while your new godly fruits will be the dominate character of Christ's relationship of love and acceptance in you. Your new traits are the evidence of your obedience and faith in your Lord. Thus your transformation accomplishes the purpose you were created for: To reflect the image of God and be His ambassador on this earth. Hallelujah!

Prayer: A Lady's Character

Dear Lord,

Please forgive me for choosing worldly characters as my habit to survive. I have used these coping mechanisms long enough to get what I wanted in life. But now I know that it is not the character that you had for me. Help me Lord to see my character as you originally designed me to be. I want Your nature of righteousness and holiness to dwell in my heart.

Change me Lord, and give me a renewed mind as in Romans 12:2. Assist me to align myself to Your Word and to receive my new character in Christ.

Thank You for the favor of Your love and transformation in my life. Thank You for the repentance of my heart toward Your character and the forsaking of my worldly character choices. My song sings out to you in worship Lord, saying, "Please make me like you Lord, do what you must do, you are a servant Lord, please make me one too." In the mighty name of Jesus I pray. Amen!

Group Discussion: Your Character

1. What is God doing in you to change your character to match His?

2. Do you notice how God takes time to develop you into what He wants you to be? How long has it taken you to agree with God's magnificent work in you? Why?

3. Where is your level of trust with God in giving you a new character reputation? Are you allowing Him to enter into your heart to do surgery? In what ways?

4. What are your challenges in building your spiritual character in Christ? Share your story with the group.

5. Are you ready to forgive yourself of your old character traits? Would you receive God's new character as your new grace? Which characters of His do you want?

6. Have you ever felt that you missed out on something great because you chose fear, anger, or rejection as your friends instead of God? What did it feel like as you sat with these characters?

"Don't worry about anything;
instead, pray about everything; tell God your needs,
and don't forget to thank him for his answers."
(Philippians 4:6 TLB)

8

HER PRAYERS

A LADY PRESENTS HER PRAYERS TO GOD.
SHE KNOWS HER MESSAGE IS A SWEET SMELLING AROMA TO HIM.

A Lady bows her knees and honors her Lord with her prayers. For a Lady, the most natural Christian instinct is to pray. She presents her prayers as a sweet smelling aroma unto the Lord knowing that each word is received as a beautiful scent beyond compare. Ephesians 5:2 verifies that Christ's love for us is a sweet fragrance to God's nostrils: *"…And God was pleased, for Christ's love for you was like sweet perfume to him."* A Lady loves that He breathes in each of her appeals and delights in responding to every one of her needs. With great expectation at what He will do, she reaches out to God to talk to Him about every circumstance she has. She keeps her heart open to listen to His answers and she knows without a doubt that He is her beloved God who responds with great pleasure to her urgent cries.

A Lady may keep a prayer journal, in easy reach. She may place it by her bed for when her beloved calls in the wee hours of the morning. She doesn't mind being awakened because His presence is such a welcome expression of His tender communion with her. His words melt away her loneliness and sorrow, turning her thoughts toward Him.

She may sit in prayer for hours but she is not concerned, as her time with Him stops the hands of the clock. A Lady knows that God hears the prayers of the righteous and that He always answers. The answer may not always match our desires but they never fail to be His perfect will for our benefit.

Prayer Is Talking To God

Yes, prayer is simply talking and communicating with God. It is a venture to plainly speak what is on your mind or in your heart. You don't have to hold back anything, even your silly phrases are dear to God. Talking to Him is a moment-by-moment happening, communicating with Him as you go about your day. You might compare it with our modern times, where so many of us are continually texting, Facebooking, Twittering or e-mailing one another. We love to chat or sometimes even chatter. Parents can scarcely get their tweens and teens to stop this compulsion. Prayer, too, is a continual and intimate dialogue—chatting as treasured friends, sweethearts or married partners do. In these relationships, we continually talk just to touch each other with words, waiting to hear each other's answers. At its most perfect, prayer is agreeing with God about what He already wants to do in our lives.

The Five Types of Prayer

Prayer is a way to seek God's attention by crying out to Him; to demonstrate your emotions, to *tell it all* from your heart with an open heart for hearing His response. It is a time of honesty to request favor from God, seeking His actions and answers.

You can talk to Him about what you want or need—this is called *petition*. You can confess to Him your shortcomings and failures—this is *confession*. You can praise Him with adoration—this is called *praise*. You can express gratitude to Him for answering your prayers or providing for some special need—this is called *thankfulness*. You can take authority, executing judgment against the enemy—this is called *deliverance*. And you can pray for the purposes and welfare of others—this is called *intercession*. Let's discover some details about each of these types of prayers.

♥ **Prayers of Petition**
A prayer of petition is the simple, straightforward act of asking for something that you want. 1 John 5:14-15 tells us, *"Now this is the confidence that we have in Him, that if we ask anything according to His will, He hears us. And if we know that He hears us, whatever we*

ask, we know that we have the petitions that we have asked of Him." Mark 11:24 confirms this to us stating, *"Therefore I say to you, whatever things you ask when you pray, believe that you receive them, and you will have them."* This is our great assurance, granted from God's Word: If we pray, He will answer! His Word tells us He is not going to answer according to *our will* but we are guaranteed that He will answer them according to *His will.* James 4:2-3 explains to us, *"And yet the reason you don't have what you want is that you don't ask God for it. And even when you do ask you don't get it because your whole aim is wrong—you want only what will give you pleasure"* (TLB). As you pray His Word to Him you will receive the petitions of your heart. Reminding God of His Word in prayer is aligning your will with His.

Tell of a time when God answered your prayers of Petition.

_____

_____

_____

_____

_____

_____

We may pray and ask but not often receive what we have asked for. Receiving is not the same thing as having—it is praying, believing by faith, accepting that it has been given by God and then thanking Him for it. You then grant Him time to bring it to you. *Having* is about His time-table. *Receiving* is about your faith in God. Let's say that you have a need for forgiveness. You pray, you ask for forgiveness, you receive the provision of forgiveness and then you thank God for it. Then you wait for Him to bring it solidly into your heart. Through faith and knowing your request aligns with Scripture, you are confident that He has given it to you. Now, the heart-change of remorse and true sorrow of forgiveness will come as God's transforming power works in your heart. In the meantime, you have received the provision of forgiveness through faith. Remember, faith is a belief in or a confident attitude toward God.

The first bible presented to me when I was saved was "The Open Bible." It has been a friend to me all these years and I would like to share with you one of my favorite study notes from it:

> *"We must admit our sins, regret the actions of our sin, plead the blood of Christ, and believe that God has indeed done what He promised, namely, to cleanses us from sin and restore us to fellowship and service."* [3]

Do you receive what you ask for in prayer? Why or why not?

_____

_____

_____

_____

_____

_____

♥ Prayers of Confession

Confession is simply admitting the truth to God. It means to agree with Him that He and His ways are right. Honesty is the key to the prayer of confession.

Psalm 51 is truly a guide for any Christian to follow when confession is warranted. King David begins his prayer by openly and freely admitting his sin. He eventually displays real sorrow for his sin, demonstrating his remorse and godly sorrow. He asks for forgiveness and then believes that God heard his prayer. He is sure that God will restore him because he knows the truth of God's character of mercy. He acknowledges that all God wants is a broken spirit and a contrite heart...not sacrifice of deeds, penitence or suffering.

It is a good practice to say confession prayers daily because we are not able to go through life without sinning each day. Unconfessed sin can weigh you down and put a wall between you and God. Here is a short list of the many ways we may sin without even realizing we are sinning:

anger	fearfulness	guilt	disappointment
shame	unforgiveness	bitterness	pridefulness
arrogance	rejection	control	manipulation

Every time you recognize these spirits at work, you know it is time to pray a prayer of confession and mean it from your heart.

We allow these negative spirits to lead our lives and use them to control others. God's Word permits us to be angry but we are commanded to *"...settle our hearts before the day ends or the devil can get a foot hold in your life"* (Eph 4:26). If you allow the anger to last more than a day then a whole group of other spirits can join with anger such as unforgiveness, bitterness, pride and arrogance and can become a stronghold in your heart. The Lord reminds us that He will have *"...no other gods before Him"* (Exodus 20:1-3). Anger and all other negative spirits are "other gods" that we set before our Lord Jesus. Therefore, we need to clear our hearts with prayers of confession, get back into God's Spirit again and conduct our lives with godliness, righteousness and holiness. Ecclesiastes 7:9 reminds us, *"Do not hasten in your spirit to be angry, for anger rests in the bosom of fools."*

Sin hinders your relationship with God and may keep your prayers from being answered. It always results in separation between you and God bringing a division of truth. 1 John 1:9 tells us that we will be forgiven and cleansed from our sins through confession: *"If we confess our sins, He is faithful and just to forgive us our sins and to cleanse us from all unrighteousness."* God is a man of His Word. Therefore, begin to pray your prayers of confession and see what restoration God will bring upon your life.

What prayers of confession do you need to say?

🖉 _____

_____

_____

_____

_____

_____

♥ **Prayers of Praise**
Praising the Lord is simply acknowledging His attributes as our God. The Psalms are full of prayers of praise. They ring out with adoration towards God and sing honor to His character and accomplishments. David writes in Psalm 103, *"I bless the holy name of God with all my heart. Yes, I will bless the Lord and not forget the glorious things he does for me. He forgives all my sins. He heals me. He ransoms me from hell. He surrounds me with loving-kindness and tender mercies. He fills my life with good things! My youth is renewed like the eagle's! He gives justice... He revealed his will and nature...He is merciful and tender...He is slow to get angry...He never bears a grudge...He has not punished us...He has removed our sins...He is like a father to us...He knows we are but dust...Let everything everywhere bless the Lord. And how I bless him too!"* (TLB)

Truly, after reading this exaltation of Psalms 103 you can clearly see that this is a prayer of praise and adoration to God. David acknowledges every aspect of the personal benefits given to him by God through claiming what God did for him. We are to humbly praise Him, just like David did, for who He is—Lord of all!

There are also a few Psalms about *how* to praise God. For example, *"We shall praise God in His sanctuary, for His mighty heavens, for His powerful acts, and His abundant greatness. We shall praise Him with the trumpet blast, the harp and lyre, with tambourine and dance, with flute and strings, with resounding cymbals, and with clashing cymbals. Let everything that has breath praise the Lord"* (Psalms 150). As you can see, praising can be an expression that is also quite loud! Now, perhaps you were raised in a church tradition that did not have a praise band, or even any music at all, and was very solemn about praise. That's fine. I'm just showing you what the Word of God says about the matter. Reverence most certainly has its place, in and out of church services. However, there's no denying that our spiritual forefathers made some noise and that God approved.

I remember when my older grandchildren were small. I used to get out the pan lids and wooden spoons. We would dance around the house waving scarves, clanging pan lids and proclaiming, "Jesus is Lord!" It was a good day when we praised the Lord in this fashion. It drew us to the Lord and made His presence near. We delighted in our time of praise. It made me feel like a real Lady, one who demonstrated the importance of praising God and acknowledging Him as Lord of my life.

Psalms 147:1 declares, *"Praise the Lord! For it is good to sing praises to our God; For it is pleasant, and praise is beautiful."*

Tell of your praises for your Lord:

✎ _____

_____

_____

_____

♥ Prayers of Thankfulness

Being thankful is a godly response to God's blessings toward us. Our gratitude in prayers of thanksgiving demonstrates our relationship with Him as a giver and us as a receiver. The most precious blessing given to us was His Son, Jesus, for which we have many reasons to be thankful.

We are to come close to our Lord with thankfulness in everything. Psalm 100 tells us how to enter into His presence through this approach. This is the Biblical way to come near to Him with your wants and needs, *"Make a joyful* **shout** *to the Lord, all you lands! Serve the Lord with* **gladness***; Come before His presence with* **singing***.* **Know** *that the Lord, He is God; It is He who has made us, and not we ourselves; We are His people and the sheep of His pasture. Enter into His gates with* **thanksgiving***, and into His courts with* **praise***.* **Be thankful** *to Him, and* **bless** *His name. For the Lord is good; His mercy is everlasting, and His truth endures to all generations"* (Psalm 100, emphasis mine). Can you see the bolded Words prompting you with ways of approaching God? Isn't it marvelous how intimate we can be with God—singing, shouting, being glad, knowing for sure that He is our God, being thankful, praising Him and blessing Him. Wow! What a day we would all have if we started each day like this.

Our country's forefathers clearly understood the powerful act of thanksgiving, as evidenced in our nation's traditional celebration of a day of thanksgiving each year. As we acknowledge that day, our prayers of thanksgiving reach the heavens and are breathed-in by our Lord. Our country's hope is that He hears our thanks for all He has given to us and in return, He is pleased by our humble gratitude toward Him.

1 Thessalonians 5:18 tells us, *"In everything give thanks; for this is the will of God in Christ Jesus for you."* Here are some reasons to be thankful: your redemption, your salvation, God's mercy and grace toward you, the provision of forgiveness given to us by Jesus' death, your spiritual restoration, your reconciliation to God and others, your family, relatives, friends, church, your personal needs, your marriage, your children and all of your

needs being met. Give thanks for all of your material blessings, God's nature surrounding you, your possessions and all spiritual blessings. Your health and emotional wellness, your abilities, gifts and your talents should be on this list too. Even your ministries, wisdom, understanding, the weather, your job, your purpose in life and your soul's prosperity, are also included—and the list goes on-and-on. We are even to be thankful for our many trials and afflictions as they produce patience, which produces character. *"When we run into problems and trials, for we know that they are good for us-they help us learn to be patient. And patience develops strength of character in us and helps us trust God more each time we use it until finally our hope and faith are strong and steady"* (Romans 5:3-4 TLB). The realization is that we have much to be thankful for to God. So, pray a prayer of thankfulness today and cultivate an *attitude* of *gratitude*!

Write your prayers of thankfulness here:

_____

_____

_____

_____

_____

_____

_____

_____

♥ **Prayers of Intercession**
To intercede means to pray to God for the purposes and benefits of another person's life and needs. We, as chosen servants of God, are called to labor in prayer for the purposes

of the kingdom and for others. Our serving in intercessory prayer should bring about changes in people, our nation, government, jobs, temptations and the supernatural circumstances. A servant begins by asking requests of God so others will prosper. Here are some requests that you might ask of God in intercession:

♥ Assurance	♥ Knowledge
♥ Bold Witnessing	♥ Love
♥ Christian Fruit	♥ Loyalty
♥ Conviction of sin	♥ Mercy
♥ Deliverance	♥ Obedience
♥ Diligence	♥ Patience
♥ Endurance	♥ Peace
♥ Faith	♥ Preservation
♥ Faithfulness	♥ Provision of Needs
♥ Forgiveness	♥ Purity
♥ Generosity	♥ Right Conduct
♥ Grace	♥ Right Motive
♥ Healing	♥ Spiritual Cleansing
♥ Holiness	♥ Spiritual Growth
♥ Hope	♥ Stewardship
♥ Humility	♥ Understanding
♥ Integrity	♥ Unity
♥ Joy	♥ Wisdom
♥ Justice	♥ Zealousness

Interceding and praying for someone else is a selfless act of kindness. Jesus went before His Father and prayed as He hung on the cross while in agony over His own physical and spiritual situation: "...*Father, forgive them, for they do not know what they do*"

(Luke 23:34). He was concerned about the condition of the two criminals who hung on their cross beside Him. Even at the very edge of His own death, Jesus was interceding for other's benefits. He had a heart of compassion and was people-minded instead of self-minded. Stephen, the Apostle, made intercession at the time of his death also. As he was being stoned to death, the Bible recorded him kneeling down and saying in Acts 7:60, *"Then he knelt down and cried out with a loud voice, Lord, do not charge them with this sin."* He was asking God to forgive the people of his imminent murder. Do you think you could cry out with this same request while someone is attempting to murder you? A mature believer intercedes with selfless compassion by petitioning God for another person's needs and provisions when it is brought to her attention.

Apostle Paul writes in 1 Timothy 2:1-3: *"Here are my directions: Pray much for others; plead for God's mercy upon them; give thanks for all he is going to do for them. Pray in this way for kings and all others who are in authority over us, or are in places of high responsibility, so that we can live in peace and quietness, spending our time in godly living and thinking much about the Lord. This is good and pleases God our Savior"* (TLB). God makes it pretty plain that we are called to intercede for others.

Write your prayer of intercession for someone who needs prayer.

_____

_____

_____

_____

The Bottom Line of Prayer – Intimacy

A song from the 1940's went like this: "Getting to know you, getting to know more about you, getting to like you, getting to hope you like me." This song is a theme of intimacy. The ultimate aspiration of prayer is to promote intimacy with God and to tell Him all about what you are thinking, where you are emotionally, what is heavy on your heart, and how you would like Him to get involved. Intimacy can be interpreted just the way it is pronounced—in-to-me-see: a looking into the depths of your inner heart and revealing what deep dark secrets are kept there. Intimacy is about opening the door of your heart and letting everything fall out, without the awful *"aaaaaahhh"* of fright or distrust that someone saw the inner core you were trying to shield, hide, or avoid. It is a willingness to allow God to know you in a deeper way and the development of a familiar closeness in relationship with Him as your best friend. Proverbs 18:24 reminds us of the intimacy of one who is closer than a brother, *"There are 'friends' who pretend to be friends, but there is a friend who sticks closer than a brother"* (TLB).

Intimacy encourages the occasion for you to take down the walls and let in the light of Christ. It is a choice to allow Him to know you so well that there are not any unrevealed secrets between the two of you. In true intimacy, there is only pure love, the kind of love that doesn't hold back or hide anything—all is out in the open and uncovered.

Intimacy helps lead to the development of trust. It is evident when you don't fear telling Him any of your secrets because you know that He will not condemn you, yell at you, beat you up verbally, or batter you physically. He won't snap at you, hate you, throw you out, or shame you. You can count on His character so well that you are assured of your safety and protection around Him. Therefore, you can trust that His response will not harm or hurt you. His gentleness is a proven response over and over again. Therefore, you can trust and depend on His steady character of faithfulness. He sees into you and you see into Him.

Prayer: A Lady's Prayers

Dear Precious Lord,

I ask that You teach me to pray according to Your will:
    to petition You for my every need and purpose
    to be thankful to You for what You have done
    to confess to You my sins with honesty
    to praise You at all times
    to intercede for other's needs

Lord, hear the cry of my heart to learn to pray at all times. Only You can train me in these ways. Holy Spirit, convict me to pray for the needs of others and to identify my own needs bringing them to You quickly and responsibly. Please make me a prayer warrior according to Your will. In Jesus name I pray, Amen.

Group Discussion: Your Prayers

1. First Thessalonians 5:16-18 tells us: *Rejoice always, pray without ceasing, in everything give thanks; for this is the will of God in Christ Jesus for you.* How can you apply these instructions to your life?

2. Are you prepared to truly be a friend to God and develop a relationship with Him through prayer?

3. What prayer type is your favorite mode of prayer? Petition? Confession? Thankfulness? Praise? Intercession? Why?

4. Do you have a regular prayer time and place? Share your favorite prayer details with the group.

5. How do you perceive that you can have more prayer time? Are you willing to commit to more prayer?

6. Are you trusting God to answer your prayers as you pray? Why? Why not?

*"Be gentle and ready to forgive; never hold grudges.
Remember, the Lord forgave you,
so you must forgive others."
(Colossians 3:13 TLB)*

HER FORGIVENESS

A LADY IS FORGIVING TOWARD HERSELF AND OTHERS.
SHE ABIDES BY THE COMMAND TO FORGIVE.

Forgiveness seems so impossible when a Lady doesn't fully understand why she must forgive someone who caused such emotional or physical harm to her. "But this was an act of destruction and devastation in my life," she says. When God commanded her to forgive He must have had a valid reason for her to do this. Mark 11:25-26 appeals to us, *"And whenever you stand praying, if you have anything against anyone, forgive him that your Father in heaven may also forgive you your trespasses. But if you do not forgive, neither will your Father in heaven forgive your trespasses."* A Lady's task is to recognize the importance of this command from her Heavenly Father and to be quick to obey. She is encouraged to know she can rely on her precious Lord for strength and comfort, realizing she cannot forgive without His help. This may be the most difficult part of a Lady's spiritual journey. The path can be full of brambles and rocks to stumble over, but God's promises and Jesus' perfect example can be the lamp for her feet.

Forgiveness is Not a Choice

When the Word speaks to us about forgiveness, it is made clear that this matter is weighty and urgent on the heart of our God. Forgiveness is the precise provision that Christ's death gave to you. He paid a price so you could live abundantly beyond your sin and failures.

The price He paid was dear. And the resulting forgiveness stands as the unfailing solution to the problem of sin. The Apostle Peter wisely warns us in Romans 6:23 that *"The wages of sin is death,"* but the good news is, *"He has delivered us from the power of darkness and conveyed us into the kingdom of the Son of His love, in whom we have redemption through His blood, the forgiveness of sins"* (Col 1:13-14).

In order for us to walk in the blessed gift of forgiveness, we need to understand it. To help us, God commands us over and over again to practice forgiveness in our daily lives, going as far as to tell us that our own forgiveness is dependent upon our forgiving others! That is obviously much more than a simple request. Sweet Lady, this is not so that those who have offended you can get away without a penalty—it is for your great benefit (so you can experience and live by Christ's example) and so that you may be an instrument of grace, bringing others to a saving knowledge of Christ through your actions. God's command is a beautiful display of the magnitude of His love for you. Therefore, as He forgives you, you are to forgive others.

Whom to Forgive

Now that we understand how important the matter of forgiveness is to God, let's take a look at who needs your forgiveness. You may be surprised to discover areas of your heart that are holding onto unforgiveness.

♥ Forgive God

How many times do we blame God for things like: "Why did my child have to die," "Why did he take my husband," "Why was my child abused," or, "Why did this accident have to happen?" Yes, there are many "whys" that linger in our minds about God and His ways. The fact is, He is God and we are not. So, we cannot expect to know or understand all that He does. However, we are to give Him our complete trust and firmly hold to the belief that God is good and will do good for us all the time. Admittedly, God does not need to be forgiven but you need the practice of releasing your heart from unforgiveness plus the experience of humbleness to obey Him. Scripture confirms to us, *"If we confess our sins, He is faithful and just to forgive us our sins and to cleanse us from all unrighteousness. If we say that we have not sinned, we make Him a liar, and His word is not in us"* (1 John 1:9-10). When you forgive God, you release yourself from the heavy burden of resentment, hatred and bitterness. In that process, you will also discover restored joy and more intimate fellowship with God.

♥ **Forgive Others**

How many friends, family members or even acquaintances around you have hurt you deeply? How many have out-right offended you or broken your heart, causing emotional wounding and crushing devastation to your soul? Your list may include husbands, boyfriends, mothers, fathers, siblings, children, teachers, pastors, or friends. They all have crossed your path and left footprints on your heart and they all need your forgiveness as much as you need to forgive them.

When Jesus taught the disciples the perfect way to pray, His "Lord's Prayer" only contained one phrase that was conditional and more than a request. You will recognize, *"forgive our sins just as we have forgiven those who have sinned against us"* (Matt 6:12 TLB).

Forgiveness is the key to re-establishing your heart concerning others. When you step before God and confess that you will forgive these people who have hurt you, you are settling your heart and positioning yourself to re-enter abundant life again. This act of confessed forgiveness leaves your heart free to love again and also to begin to trust again.

♥ **Forgive Yourself**

How many times have you put off forgiving yourself when you really should have done this years ago? Forgiveness is part of the unmerited favor that God gave you when you received Christ as your Savior. He wants you to regard yourself the same way that you are regarded by Him.

Let's establish the principle of forgiveness:

As you were brought into the kingdom of God
at your Salvation,
you received God's grace to be forgiven.

Self-forgiveness does not always come easily. Because of Satan's influence, we can sometimes believe that our sin is too severe to be forgiven or that we don't deserve to be forgiven. If we allow ourselves that indulgence, we then become captives of spiritual strongholds and have forgotten the truth that sets us free. In fact, John 8:36 declares, *"Therefore if the Son makes you free you shall be free indeed."* By God's grace, you have been forgiven and are called to receive His grace fully.

Recognizing Your Unforgiveness

It is possible to believe you have forgiven when you really have not let go of your sense of offense. I have listed below a few examples of how we may use coping mechanisms to avoid confronting our unforgiveness. Notice methods of manipulation and a host of spirits we can operate in when trying to "stay in control." Do you recognize yourself anywhere on this list?

♥ You move into the background to "scope things out."
  suspiciousness

♥ You have to be right as much as possible.
  fear of embarrassment/perfectionism

♥ You remind others of their failures.
  accusations

♥ You lock others out of your heart when they disappoint you.
  rejection

♥ You change your plans constantly to keep others off track.
  dominance/mistrust

♥ You use denial to stay in control.
  unyielding/unsubmitted

♥ You fight the call to surrender.
  manipulation

When we harbor unforgiveness in our hearts, we may engage in self-destructive behaviors like drug and alcohol abuse, promiscuity, self-abuse, rebellion, rage or attempted suicide. God is offering you the chance to surrender the pain that continues to hurt you. In fact, He is offering to fight your enemies for you! In 2 Corinthians 10:3-4 we learn how to war God's way: *"It is true that I am an ordinary, weak human being, but I don't use human plans and methods to win my battles. I use God's mighty weapons, not those made by men, to knock down the devil's strongholds"* (TLB). I hear you asking, "So what are God's weapons for my personal battles?" The answer is: Confession, forgiveness and repentance. These break the yoke of bondage and help to bring you back into the presence of the Lord. Unforgiveness closes the door of God's presence and keeps you from entering His courts. However, forgiveness empties your heart and sets you right in the middle of His heavenly chambers again.

The Truth and The Lies About Forgiveness

Forgiveness is based on the love our Heavenly Father has for us. It is the main ingredient of His character. He commands us to forgive because He understands that ongoing entanglements with strongholds of unforgiveness can rob us of our destiny. On the other hand, true forgiveness can set us free from this bondage.

The deception of Satan is subtle and often very convincing to our limited mind. We cannot see things the way God can see them, nor are we always aware of Satan's tactics that lead us to sin unless the Holy Spirit reveals them to us. Proverbs 10:12 lets us know that, *"Hatred stirs old quarrels, but love overlooks insults."* We were created with the ability to choose so we could be in relationship with God. In all His ways, He implores: *"choose forgiveness."*

There are times you may feel you have forgiven someone when you really haven't had a genuine change of heart. So, it may come as a surprise when you find yourself easily offended by that same person in the future. To help you understand and choose wisely, we're going to lay out some basic truths and lies about forgiveness. There's a table on the next page that should help you identify areas where you may need to put in a few extra minutes of prayer that may lead to praise one day. Why don't you get out your highlighter for this one, dear Lady!

The Lies	The Truth
I don't need to forgive. It's over—just forget about it. This is an act of obedience. Forgetting is not forgiving. God commands active participation from your heart to release your offender.	*Forgiving is giving up my vengeance against the offender.* God promises that He will handle the process of vengeance. Our job is to forgive and trust His ways of justice with others.
When I forgive, I am reconciled with my offender. Reconciliation takes two willing people. You can forgive all by yourself and the offender may not even be aware in some cases.	*When I continue in unforgiveness, I don't hurt the offender, I hurt myself.* There is a popular saying that, "Unforgiveness is the poison we drink hoping the other person will die." It erodes your soul and robs your joy.
When I forgive, my painful memories will instantly go away. Time is key in memories. You are called to forgive quickly, but you may still feel some pain until your healing is complete.	*When someone sins against me, I don't have to be unforgiving in return.* Be careful not to be affected by the sins of others. Stay forgiving, fighting against temptation to sin.

Taking The First Step

Pain is usually the first indication that forgiveness needs to take place. But how do we begin? Expressing your pain to God can be a great way of getting the ball rolling. But don't stop at venting. Learn to keep moving forward through the stages of progress by first expressing yourself with your tears and crying out, then admitting you are hurting and acknowledging you have been wounded. Then, ask your Heavenly Father to help you forgive your offender. He will always provide, by the Holy Spirit, conviction to forgive when you ask for it. You may think that staying separate from the pain or stuffing will bring your healing. However, God won't let you skirt around the process of forgiveness. He wants your heart to be totally healed. A loving,

Heavenly Father doesn't want you to be condemned to the prison of unforgiveness and bitterness for the rest of your life. His compassion for you is merciful and kind. He wants you to be released from the bondage of continual sin. As you read and learn God's Word, you will be given ample opportunity to realize that you are sinning while operating in unforgiveness. Eventually, God will show you that all of His commands are for *your* benefit and you will know the joy of genuine forgiveness.

If you would like to have forgiveness and restoration from your sin of unforgiveness, then ask God to forgive you, especially where you may be expecting to somehow pay for your own sin. Then, simply humble yourself and repent (turn from your ways toward God's ways), allowing Jesus to pay your price as you surrender your unforgiveness to Him. He will take your sin and redeem you from the penalty of the law. Therefore, you will be able to walk in true redemptive forgiveness with yourself in God's state of grace. Psalms 32:3-5 says, *"When I kept silent, my bones grew old through my groaning all the day long. For day and night Your hand was heavy upon me; My vitality was turned into the drought of summer...I acknowledged my sin to You, and my iniquity I have not hidden. I said, "I will confess my transgressions to the Lord," and You forgave the iniquity of my sin."*

Continuing on The Path

You will have opportunities to quickly forgive offenses of all shapes and sizes on a daily basis. Even if you're still working on forgiving those who have hurt you most, you can win small victories whenever the opportunity presents itself. To measure your progress in the area of forgiveness, keep 2 Corinthians 13:5-6 at hand, which tells us to check the condition of our hearts to see if we are truly following Christ: *"Check up on yourselves. Are you really Christians? Do you pass the test? Do you feel Christ's presence and power more and more within you? Or are you just pretending to be Christians when actually you aren't at all"* (TLB). Are you believing God's will for your life by relinquishing your unforgiveness to Him? Lamentations 3:40-42 tells us to repent and turn to the Lord in honesty, *"Let us examine ourselves instead, and let us repent and turn again to the Lord. Let us lift our hearts and hands to him in heaven, for we have sinned; we have rebelled against the Lord"* (TLB).

Pondering these scriptures may help strengthen your mind and your will about harboring unforgiveness. Surrendering your will and accepting the truth of God's will is the powerful choice that will set you free. It is a complete surrender, acknowledging that He is Lord and giving Him permission to remove anything that doesn't look like Him. Psalm 51:12 says, *"Restore to me again the joy of your salvation, and make me willing to obey you"* (TLB). When you surrender, you tell God that you have tried all that you could to make the pain go away and now you are willing to let Him have this pain which was His desire in the first place.

Your biggest challenge will always be areas that you do not want to change. Therefore, your willingness to obey God's Word is your key to success here. Do you trust enough to forgive or do you believe that you can settle the situation on your own and become self-justified? Which will it be – an act of obedience to forgive or will you use your own self-will and get your own outcome *again*?

You must remember that seeking the will of your Heavenly Father in forgiveness invites new ways for trust to develop in your heart. Your old habits will not work in God's Kingdom. You have to do things His way. Proverb 28:13 reminds us of consequences for not obeying God's ways, *"He who covers his sins will not prosper, but whoever confesses and forsakes them will have mercy."* Your willingness to trust tells your Heavenly Father that you are ready to begin to conform to His will for your life.

Prayer: A Lady's Forgiveness

Dear Heavenly Father,

Please forgive me for believing that I could pay the debt for my own sins. I have overlooked the objective of Christ's death and looked to my own means to resolve my sin. Now, I can forgive myself even though others may not want to forgive me. I simply chose to forgive by placing my sin under the blood of Jesus and walking free. I am in alignment with Your bounty for me. Freedom is a place of liberty, out from under the condemnation of the law and into Your grace.

Thank you, Lord, for covering me with Jesus' blood. It has set me free and now that I am free I choose to forgive all others who have hurt me or stepped on my heart and caused me pain. I forgive each person (____name them____) and release them from having to pay a price that they too could not pay. I will let You have Your way with them because I release them over to You. I thank You for my forgiveness and my freedom from unforgiveness. I shall follow Your commands to forgive for the rest of my life. In the mighty name of Jesus, I pray. Amen.

Group Discussion: Your Forgiveness

1. Have you considered forgiveness as your path to freedom and liberty to mature in Christ?

2. Do you practice forgiveness daily? How can you introduce it into your everyday life if you are not confessing forgiveness daily?

3. Who in your life do you need to consider forgiving? Please share these stories with others in your group?

4. How long have you been holding on to bitterness and grudges against others? Would you like to surrender these sins over to God? Why? Why not?

5. Do you struggle at forgiving quickly? How can you become more aware of your unforgiveness?

6. Do you trust Jesus by surrendering your pain to Him? What pain would you like to give to Him?

SECTION IV

A LADY'S CONVICTIONS

*"Do not let your adornment be merely outward —
arranging the hair, wearing gold, or putting on fine apparel —
rather let it be the hidden person of the heart,
with the incorruptible beauty of a gentle and quiet spirit,
which is very precious in the sight of God."
(1 Peter 3:3-4)*

❧10❧

HER FEMININITY

A LADY ACKNOWLEDGES GOD'S CREATION IN HER.
SHE HONORS THE FEMININITY GOD HAS GIVEN HER.

God has given a Lady a unique and extraordinary gift to have as her own called her femininity. The Living Bible describes a women's femininity in this way: *"Be beautiful inside, in your hearts, with the lasting charm of a gentle and quiet spirit that is so precious to God"* (TLB). However there is quite a different image of femininity in today's world. If a Lady were to form herself after the television or magazine ads or after popular singers or actors, she would be displaying an outer identity of worldly femininity. Therefore, a Lady in God's Kingdom knows the difference between worldly femininity and godly femininity. She chooses carefully which one she will actively engage.

The Two Views Of Femininity

God created us male and female, most clearly distinguished by our gender. However, our culture has embraced a blurring of these lines so that Ladies may appear quite masculine, while men seem to take on feminine attributes. Let's take a closer look.

♥ **The World's View.** The world often translates femininity as the outward demonstration of her attractiveness without looking deeper than the surface. The way a woman dresses or wears her hair conveys to the world how she would like to be perceived. In some cases, a woman may hide or disguise her outward loveliness and in other cases she may expose her feminine appearance in quite a bold way. However, each extreme is a worldly display that either over-emphasizes or under-emphasizes her genuine femininity.

♥ **The Biblical View.** In biblical terms, a Lady's femininity is her elegant self-confidence, her far-reaching patience, her soft nurturing ways, her tenderness and gentleness. Her femininity also is her quick submission, her quiet surrender and all of the godly aspects designating her Christ-likeness. These inward features demonstrate a much purer femininity than any pretty dress or shade of lipstick can suggest. The truly feminine Lady has the heart of God and lives out the customs of Christ's submission.

The Development of The Woman

When God made Eve from the rib of Adam he made her as a complement to Adam. Together as one, they made a complete reflection of God who is neither male nor female. (Gen 1:27). Eve was uniquely designed from Adam's rib and not of dust from the earth like Adam. The woman was the finishing touch of God's creation, designed to respond, as a companion, helper, and complement to Adam. The Bible says God's own character is given to the woman. (Gen 1:26). In her marriage relationship she was designed to carry out the role of the "responding helper" and her virtues are vital to the successful fulfillment of God's design for her, her marriage, and her family. This function is not to be confused with her worth or value as a woman – she was not created inferior to the man. Proverbs 31:10 tells us, *"Her worth is far above rubies"* which means that her contribution as a woman is valuable and she has an immeasurable and precious worth to God that reaches far beyond riches.

Modern History—The Present Deception

In today's world there is much controversy over the *choice to be feminine* or the *choice to be masculine*. Although our gender characteristics are clearly different and so obvious, there is confusion among our present generations.

Satan's deceptions and lies have tried to convince our generations that they may willfully chose to select another gender as their identity. They are deceived when they try to change their outward appearance and conduct themselves as someone they truly are not. Despite their desire to have a choice, God hard-wired their bodies according to His perfect plan. Our gender was chosen for us. When we deny this, we are denying God's will and His decision for our greatness within that gender.

God desires true intimacy with each of us, and only you and He were there when He made the choice to form you. Psalms 139:13-16 confirms His presence at that precious time, *"You made all the delicate, inner parts of my body and knit them together in my mother's womb... You were there while I was being formed in utter seclusion! You saw me before I was born and scheduled each day of my life before I began to breathe. Every day was recorded in your book"* (TLB)! This Scripture supplies a full description of God forming us in our mother's womb and configuring our inner parts—including our gender.

There are some choices that we have been given by God and there are choices that God has kept for himself and does not release to us. It is only through our salvation in Christ that are we able to acknowledge our true identity clearly (see Chapter 3). Christ's sacrifice conquered the father of the lies and deceptions about gender and brought forth the truth. If you are struggling with confusion in this area of your life, may I suggest that you seek counsel from a Pastor, a Christian Counselor, or a Minister who can help you discover who you are in Christ and perhaps help you find a group that can provide support.

Biblical Proclamation—Don't Follow The World's Ways

The Apostle Paul reminds us in Romans 12:2 that we are not to be squeezed into the mold of the worldly way but we are to shape our minds from God's Word which says, *"Don't copy the behavior and customs of this world...then you will learn from your own experience how His ways will really satisfy you"* (TLB). We are being warned here not to be misled by the worldly perceptions that can invade our minds and confuse us. This warning applies to femininity as well as all of life's choices. Dwelling in worldly behaviors will only distract us from the truth and from fulfilling our destiny. 1 John 2:15-17 also declares, *"Do not love the world or the things in the world. If anyone loves the world, the love of the Father is not in him."* The very best choice you can make is to stay connected to God through His Word. The more you come to know His character and will, the more you'll lose your appetite for the ways of the world.

True Femininity Is "Surrender"

A Lady's assignment of obedience is centered on a life of surrender. As a woman of God, she surrenders in obedience to her Lord and Savior all throughout her life. As a single woman, she surrenders herself in a unique way for service to her God and her community. When she becomes a bride, she surrenders her life of independence to be of service to her husband. As part of this surrender, she relinquishes her name, her will to her husband's godly leadership and ultimately her body in the marriage bed. As a mother, she surrenders her life for the lives of her children and the sake of their welfare. She believes the Scriptures which tell her that she represents the excellence of the Lord, *"But a wise, understanding, and prudent wife is from the Lord"* (Prov 19:14 AMP). She is careful, sensible, practical, discreet, and wise as she seeks to be like Jesus in everything she thinks, speaks, and does.

True Femininity Is "Submission"

First and foremost, a Lady is called to submit to the authority of God. His choice for us is that we should willingly submit to Him in everything we do. A single woman submits primarily to God, while a married woman additionally submits to her husband.

Women become confused and sometimes angry about this "S" word. You may be wondering, "How and what am I expected to submit?" What God requires of a wife is to yield her opinions and views to her husband, trusting in Him, and depending on Him in the process. God's intention is for husbands to consider every morsel of information their wives have submitted to them, then make decisions according to God's commands and character. Because she has contributed in humble submission rather than simply asserting her position or making demands, her husband is released from the temptation to defend his authority. He can now focus on making better decisions for the entire family's benefit.

Ephesians 5:22-24 confirms, *"Wives, be subject (be submissive and adapt yourselves) to your own husbands as [a service] to the Lord. For the husband is head of the wife as Christ is the head of the church. Himself the Savior of [His] body. As the church is subject to Christ, so let wives also be subject to their husbands"* (AMP). This type of submission means to yield in humbleness and respect, voluntarily, without suggestion of inferiority or worthlessness, acknowledging—in an act of faith—the husband's leadership responsibilities under God.

When a Lady submits all that she has—her understanding, knowledge, opinions, feelings, and all her energies—to her husband with respect, God will prompt the husband to receive it from her and consider it valid. 1 Peter 3:1-2 says, *Wives, fit in with your husbands' plans; for then if they refuse to listen when you talk to them about the Lord, they will be won by your respectful, pure behavior. Your godly lives will speak to them better than any words* (TLB). The model of a husband and wife joined in submission to God is what creates the fertile soil for a Lady to sow her seeds of submission to her partner. 1 Peter 3:7 says, *"You husbands must be careful of your wives, being thoughtful of their needs and honoring them as the weaker sex. Remember that you and your wife are partners in receiving God's blessings, and if you don't treat her as you should, your prayers will not get ready answers"* (TLB).

Our willingness to submit to God first and then to our marriage relationship demonstrates our desire for God's will to lead our lives. Galatians 2:20 tells us that we have died with Christ, *"I have been crucified with Christ; it is no longer I who live, but Christ lives in me."* As we are dead in our worldliness (flesh) Christ now lives in us as our Spirit. Therefore, Ladies are called to not only submit to their husbands but also place themselves in positions of accountability to masters such as employers (Tit 2:9), secular authorities such as governmental rulers (Rom 13:1), and church officials such as elders (1 Pet 5:5). Of course, there are certain circumstances where it is appropriate to take a stand against abuse of authority, this should be reserved for extreme situations and not be your policy. While you may have strong feelings or urges to resist, you are a spectacular example of biblical femininity when you conduct yourself in this way. As you show respect for authority, God is glorified and others can see Him in you.

Femininity Is The Inward Beauty Of A Lady's Heart.

We opened this chapter with Peter telling us what femininity looks like in a godly Lady. Let's look once more at verse 3 of 1 Peter and again be reminded, *"Don't be concerned about the outward beauty that depends on jewelry, or beautiful clothes, or hair arrangement."* (TLB). God is asking you to demonstrate your femininity not by merely considering your outward appearance the way the rest of the world so often does, but by your reverent conduct and by displaying a heart that is, modest, respectful, honoring, appreciating, admiring, and devoted to deeply loving. You honor God by enjoying your role as a Lady. God wants you to consider His purpose for your life first and foremost, not your sex-appeal or outward appearance. Peter goes on to explain more of that charming feminine spirit that God created Ladies everywhere need to adorn themselves with:

1 Peter 3:8	Be of one mind, united in Spirit
1 Peter 3:8	Be kind to others, compassionate and tender
1 Peter 3:9	Don't repay evil for evil
1 Peter 3:10	Keep control of your tongue
1 Peter 3:10	Guard your lips from telling lies
1 Peter 3:11	Turn away from evil and do good
1 Peter 3:11	Live in peace
1 Peter 3:15	Quietly trust yourself to Christ your Lord
1 Peter 3:16	Do what is right
1 Peter 3:17	Suffer for doing good, not wrong

Titus also writes on the same feminine view, encouraging women to be discreet, reverent and a virtuous homemaker who teaches the younger women to grow in housekeeping lessons and also in the Lord. Titus 2:3-5 says to us, *"The older women likewise, that they be reverent in behavior, not slanderers, not given to much wine, teachers of good things—that they admonish the young women to love their husbands, to love their children, to be discreet, chaste, homemakers, good, obedient to their own husbands, that the word of God may not be blasphemed."* If this seems old-fashioned or uncomfortable to you, please consider the eternal, unchanging nature of the God who created you. It has been his model for perfect femininity since the beginning. God isn't subject to fashions or trends.

Why Don't We Feel Feminine?

Now let's talk about all those who say that they feel no femininity about themselves and their Lady-like value is missing. This is an often heard response among the women in the body of Christ, not just among unbelievers. Here are some other comments you might hear:

♥ "I never felt feminine because Dad wanted a boy."

♥ "Dad could only relate to my brothers, so I became like them."

♥ "My Dad raised me and never taught me 'girl things.'"

♥ "As a single parent, my Mom had no time to teach me how to be a woman."

♥ "I never felt feminine because of the way others treated me, as if I were without any value at all!"

♥ "I never felt feminine because I have never looked at myself as feminine…I have a very boyish physique."

♥ "I find myself doing all the masculine jobs around the house which detract from my femininity."

Ladies, we have an enemy who wants to rob us of our femininity and make us feel less than a Lady. He knows that if he can draw us into deception then he can hold us captive in that state of "absent femininity." Satan is his name and desolation is his game!

Listen in with me for just a moment as a young woman I know, Colleen, speaks of her struggle with femininity:

"My dad never said this but he wanted me to be a boy so I agreed to try to please him. It was an unspoken agreement we had. I never felt like a girl especially after competing in all of the masculine sports games. As I look back, I see the choices I made were to sacrifice my femininity to win my Dad's affection."

Some little girls make an inner hidden vow to be what Daddy wants them to be. This is absolutely wrong, but what do little girls know beyond their desires to acquire favor in their Dad's heart so he will love them? These little girls, as grown women, struggle at being feminine or acting like a Lady, and can remain stuck in absent femininity wondering how to become free.

A Lady in God's Kingdom understands how to get from lack of prosperity to increase: It is a matter of prayer! Prayers of confession and repentance help to remove the elements of hidden childhood vows. So here is a prayer to release yourself from captivity to this type of vow:

Dear Lord,

Please forgive me that I knowingly or unknowingly wanted to be a boy for my Daddy's sake. Although I was not a boy, I thought that I could please him by acting and looking like a boy. This was deceptive thinking. So I ask you to forgive me for this vow, to release me and to set me free from this vow forever. I want to be what you made me to be. I receive your healing from any and all deceptions of trying to be "like" a boy. Now fill me with the feminine spirit of gentleness and peacefulness so I might represent you to others as your creation of a feminine Lady. Amen

As we have discussed, God calls women to use their unfading charm of a gentle and quiet (peaceful) spirit to demonstrate their femininity. This spirit is not anxious or wrought up with anger, bitterness and disappointment but is a spirit of trust and faith that is precious in the sight of God. It forthright pronounces a Lady's incorruptible Spirit of Christ in her. So, as the Lady that God created you to be, begin to proclaim your freedom from confusion and enter into the prosperity of submission and surrender to God through prayer.

Prayer: A Lady's Femininity

Dear Lord,

Please forgive me for the times I displayed my fleshly femininity and changed my reputation from godly to worldly. A worldly appearance in not what I want as my identity. I ask You to help me to repent and turn towards a Christ-like identify in You.

I also request of You to forgive me for all of the times I dismissed my femininity and viewed myself without worth or value as a Lady. You chose a gender for me in my mother's womb – I will not be deceived of my true feminine identity in Christ. Jesus, reveal Your Spirit to me so I can learn Your ways and delight in obedience to the Father as You have shown to me in your Word.

I ask You to forgive me for my lack of submission, disobedience of not surrendering my will to Yours, my times of bitterness, anger and disappointment toward others and my ways of ignoring You. I ask You to release me from these bitter spirits and set my heart free to be a gentle and quiet spirit in all of the ways that I am called to be. Help me Lord to know how to surrender to Your will because my will gets in the way of true submission to You. Your ways are the only ways that I want to engage in. Help me to repent of the times when I want to rebel.

May I be granted the privilege to be an example to others who are younger and learning to submit to obedience. Heal me from all past rebellions and show me Your will for my future in ministering the joy of femininity to others. In the mighty name of Jesus I pray. Amen!

Group Discussion: Your Femininity

1. What is your definition of femininity?

2. What is your definition of submission?

3. Do you struggle with having a gentle and quiet spirit? In what ways? To whom?

4. What do you think God is calling you to do in obedience regarding your femininity?

5. Have you repented for your lack of surrender? Are you ready to repent presently? What will it take for you to surrender your feelings to God?

6. What lies and misconceptions are keeping you from being feminine? Have you considered praying about them?

"So that no one can speak a word of blame against you,
you are to live clean, innocent lives
as children of God in a dark world
full of people who are crooked and stubborn.
Shine out among them like beacon lights."
(Philippians 2:15 TLB)

❧11❧

HER PURITY

A LADY PRESERVES HER BODY FOR MARRIAGE.
SHE INVITES PURITY TO BE HER FRIEND.

A Lady's sexual purity is vitally important to her commitment to wholeness. She aims to please God and follow His Word of truth for her life. The desire of her heart is to remain blameless and innocent in a perverse world of sexual temptation and lust. She knows that a walk of purity is a sure-footed path. She does not want to be known as a tumbleweed blowing in the wind. She wants friendship, love and relationship but not at the price of losing her virginity in a moment of deceptive passion. She knows that *"He who walks with integrity walks securely, But he who perverts his ways will become known"* (Proverbs 10:9).

Your sexuality is an area of vulnerability that is your responsibility to guard constantly. You can choose purity through abstinence or you can be whisked away by temptation, ruining a spotless reputation and throwing yourself into a pit of no return. The Bible's truth is that there will be a price to pay, good or bad, when the choice is made. *"For which of you, intending to build a tower, does not sit down first and count the cost"* (Luke 14:28).

You are called to carefully consider the cost of momentary lust versus covenant love in marriage. Let's look at a brief comparison on the next page. Can you see your own choices clearly on one side or the other?

Lust is (Colossians 3:5)	Love is (1 Corinthians 13:4-8)
Temporary	Enduring
Selfish	Unselfish
Untrustworthy	Trustworthy
Impatient	Patient
Uncontrolled Desires	Controlled Desires
Based on Fantasy	Based on Reality
Full of Emotions	Full of Devotion
Driven by Passion	Chosen by Will
Focused on Appearance	Focused on Character
Eager to Get	Eager to Give
Set on Receiving Happiness	Set on Giving Happiness

From *"Counseling Through Your Bible Handbook"* [4]

As a Lady, your choice should always be for covenant love even when lust tries to undermine your thoughts. Like Jesus being tempted by Satan, you can take a stand on the Word of God, not veering from the truth or deviating from the righteous path. In this way you will preserve your good name, as God would want you to do, making obedience your goal.

Sexual Love

When we place our sexual desires ahead of the love of Christ, we idolize sex. We leave behind the truth that sex outside of marriage or during an adulterous affair is sin when we pursue sexual gratification and call it love. Sexual "passion" in adultery or fornication is a yearning and a craving for personal pleasure, not a thirst for honoring, protecting or cherishing another person. The Word of God concerning lustful desire says, *"Therefore put to death your members which are on the earth: fornication, uncleanness, passion, evil desire, and covetousness, which is idolatry"* (Col 3:5). This means to turn away from the lusts that our bodies are tempted to indulge in; and when we turn from sin, God is always waiting with open arms of genuine love.

Agape Love

Godly love is translated from the Greek *"agape"* which means a love that has high esteem or high regard for another person's wellbeing. This includes the desire to hold another person in respect, reverence and admiration. The Word of God concerning agape love says, *"Love suffers long and is kind; love does not envy; love does not parade itself, is not puffed up; does not behave rudely, does not seek its own, is not provoked, thinks no evil; does not rejoice in iniquity, but rejoices in the truth; bears all things, believes all things, hopes all things, endures all things. Love [agape] never fails"* (1 Cor 13:4-8). True love is not a sexual love but a love that transcends beyond our fleshly passions. It is a prevailing love, ready to die for the sake of another. Love based on sexuality can eventually fade and disappear but *agape* love through God's Spirit endures eternally. True love drives out all impostors seeking to claim they are real love. The Spirit of God's Love is reverent, unconditional and unfailing. It is the only lasting love.

God's love also expresses the essential nature and character of our Lord—*"God is love,"* says 1 John 4:8. Love can only be shown through the actions it displays. The most perfect example we have of God's love, is seen in Him giving us the gift of His only Son to pay the price for the forgiveness of our sins: *"In this is love, not that we loved God, but that He loved us and sent His Son to be the propitiation for our sins"* (1 John 4:9-10). True love is a continual demonstration of eternal love confirmed by grace and everlasting compassion. 1 John 4 continues in verse 11 completing the message of love by telling us: *"Beloved, if God so loved us, we also ought to love* [agape] *one another."* Loving one another is not a reference to *sexual* love, rather a genuine godly display of behavior toward the way Jesus loves us. It is a love that fills the heart abundantly, naturally producing a respect and consideration.

Consequences

The expression of love through sexual union was designed by God to be enjoyed as a sacred thing shared by one man and one woman who are in a covenant marriage to each other. And if you need to hear it precisely, sex outside of marriage is *forbidden*. It is a sin. A lifestyle of casual sex can wreck your self-esteem and ruin your life emotionally, spiritually, and maybe even physically, sending your life into a tailspin without you even suspecting it. Sometimes, the psychological connections we make about ourselves and sex can be confusing, so much so that when the person God intended you to marry finally arrives on the scene, you may be too damaged to receive this wonderful gift.

Many women today don't consider the negative effects of premarital sex, fornication or participation in adultery. Our culture today considers sex to be the natural pursuit of passionate pleasure and satisfaction and encourages us to grab for instant gratification every day. However, living this way has deep emotional and spiritual consequences, when women experience sexuality in ways God has strictly forbidden for our benefit and protection. The consequences of casual sex are never good, either in the short and long term. You may think you're having a great time, but you are actually being deceived. Buckle your seatbelt as we explore some of the hazards of impurity.

♥ Consequence: Emotional Damage

First, in the premarital arena, 1 Thessalonians 4:3-5 says, *"For God wants you to be holy and pure and to keep clear of all sexual sin so that each of you will marry in holiness and honor—not in lustful passion as the heathen do, in their ignorance of God and His ways"* (TLB). Many young women were fortunate to have had parents and grandparents who imparted values for their lives which they later abandoned and left behind to chase a whimsical imposter of love.

After engaging in premarital sex, these misguided women may experience feelings of guilt, embarrassment, distrust, resentment, stress, tension, depression, worthlessness and more. This price of emotional baggage can then turn inward and fester into self-hatred, self-condemnation, self-degradation, self-betrayal, and possibly self-destruction. If you know in your heart that sex outside of marriage is a violation of a specific command of God's, you also realize that, if you do it anyway, you have sinned against Him and betrayed both His and your own principles and beliefs. For those who were raised without this foundation, casual sex, at best, can only perpetuate and affirm the lie that a Lady is not worthy or can never be worthy of love.

♥ Consequence: Unhealthy Relationships

Some women believe that their agreement to have sex will help keep a relationship intact. The illusion of a committed romance can be quickly shattered when a woman's "boyfriend" drops her for another who has caught his eye. Amid the anger, hatred and self-disgust that can often come in the wake of such a disappointment, it suddenly becomes painfully obvious that giving in was not the way to keep him by her side. The enemy of her soul will use grief and heartbreak as tactics. Anger, hurt, and rejection are three more of his friends that can consume a Lady's life at a time like that.

God created a marriage covenant as an agreement to be faithful to each other—to be accountable and confess your need to receive love and understanding from each other. Your covenant agreement is a contract with God that says you and your spouse have pledged your love strictly to each other. In a non-covenant relationship, there is no foundation of faithfulness to keep you safe and protected.

♥ Consequence: Adultery

1 Thessalonians 4:6-7 says, *"And this also is God's will: that you never cheat in this matter by taking another man's wife… For God has not called us to be dirty-minded and full of lust but to be holy and clean"* (TLB). Cheating spouses often begin to feel guilty, closed off from their mates and full of mistrust, thinking, "What will I do or say if he finds out?" The anticipated argument is constantly rehearsed in the adulteress' mind which keeps her conjuring lies and sitting with the devil in his den. The enemy's objective is to keep her walking in adultery, mired in emotional and spiritual misery. That misery manifests as resentment, hatred and unforgiveness toward her husband. She finds herself disrespecting him and everything about him. Her secretiveness will cause separation and place a wedge between her and her covenant partner. Her life is spent in secrecy with a third party who is not in covenant devotion with her but in lust, sex and

empty promises mistaken for love. The living of this inward lie begins to erode her wellbeing and deteriorate her joy.

This scenario can never lead you to the place God prepared for you before you were even born. Quite the contrary! If an adulterous relationship continues, you may find your feelings of suspicion and hatred for your spouse turning inward until it is full-fledged self-loathing. Depression may take over and you may end up in a pit of dark oppression. Whether you realize it or not, you are in a spiritual battle and only a choice to obey God can lead to victory.

♥ Consequence: Moral Misery

When you betray your moral instincts and drop your guard by stepping into an extra-marital affair or premarital relationship, your actions and behaviors are misaligned with God's plan for your life. You find you have to watch every word you speak—you can't be yourself. Your misery shows itself strong in every thought, deed and behavior. God's truth says in 1 Thessalonians 4:8 *"If anyone refuses to live by these [God's] rules, he is not disobeying the rules of men but of God who gives his Holy Spirit to you"* (TLB). The one law of God's that you cannot break no matter how desperately you may try is that "you <u>will</u> reap what you sow." If you have planted immorality, you can expect a harvest of misery. Since you probably started your affair because you wanted to escape some form of misery, I hope you can see the folly in this choice. Real love, real joy and real hope are found only in God.

♥ Consequence: Spiritual Ties

Every time you have sex with a person, you form a spiritual tie, often identified as a soul-tie[5]. God intended for married partners to form this tie; (1) so that the two would *think* in agreement with their *intellect*; (2) that the two would be *emotionally connected* together through their *feelings*; (3) that the two would *choose together* the same decisions of the *will*. The intimacy of intercourse in a covenant relationship prompts a connection of understanding and agreement with each other. When the marriage is consummated the spiritual and emotional ties bring the two together as "one flesh" (Gen 2:24, Mat 19:5 Eph 5:31).

However, when you have premarital sex or commit adultery, the unfortunate consequence is that you are forming a spiritual tie with every partner you encounter in this manner. This false intimacy will pull you together forming strongholds with your sexual partners even if you are not in a relationship with them anymore. This connection or soul-tie will take you down an emotional path that you may have increasing difficulty getting off of as time passes. Most people use sex as a casual pastime without even knowing that they tie themselves spiritually to their sex partners. There is considerable danger in these affairs that goes beyond just feeling badly about yourself or about getting caught. In a covenant marriage, it is the covenant that keeps you in conformity to walk together in harmony, on a path leading toward God. Clearly if you are not walking toward Him, you are either standing still or walking away from Him. The Bible describes Satan as a devourer prowling the perimeter. If you are not under God's protective wing, you are in great peril.

First Corinthians 6:19-20 says, *"Or do you not know that your body is the temple of the Holy Spirit who is in you, whom you have from God, and you are not your own? For you were bought at a price; therefore glorify God in your body and in your spirit, which are God's."* God's instruction here Ladies is that you do not own your body—it belongs to God! Ladies, you are to surrender your bodies to *God's will* and follow His path of righteousness and purity no matter what the circumstances may seem. Just knowing the consequences spiritually should keep you on the spiritual path with Christ. (See Appendix B for instructions and prayer to break soul-ties.)

♥ Consequence: Spiritual Inversion

When a woman is presented with an invitation of sex, either through verbal or non-verbal methods of communication, the responsibility falls to her to take the leadership role and make the final decision to say no. The leadership decision *should* come from the man, who should be motivated to honor and respect the woman because he honors and respects the Lord. It is his responsibility to steer the moment away from lust, however his unwillingness to do so puts the ball in her court. This phenolmenon is known as *spiritual inversion*. This inverted position leaves the woman unsupported, vulnerable, and definitely uncovered, even if she cannot sense it at the time. Scripture tells us, *"But I want you to know that the head of every man is Christ, the head of woman is man, and the head of Christ is God"* (1 Cor 11:3-4)[6]. When the woman is unnaturally positioned as the leader, the relationship often develops in such a way that she becomes responsible for managing the man's temper, emotions, behaviors and spiritual alignment. This is a confusing place for a Lady because she is actually incapable of covering a man in these ways. Though she may long for a strong leader in her man, she may discovers she distrusts him to take the headship role which may lead her to resist or refuse to give up her perceived control, believing that he is unreliable as a leader.

If you are in a relationship, take stock to see who is leading and who is providing the headship covering for you. You have not been made nor are you equipped to handle any position other than your protected role by the man. *"You husbands must be careful of your wives, being thoughtful of their needs and honoring them as the weaker vessel. Remember that you and your wife are partners in receiving God's blessings, and if you don't treat her as you should, your prayers will not get ready answers"* (1 Peter 3:7).

♥ **Consequences: Physical Peril**
Casual affairs may seem like breezy fun at first, but they can result in unexpected pregnancy, disease, stress and possibly abuse if you haven't taken the time to get to know your partner well enough. The hazards are many and the cost is high for making the decision to say, "yes" to immoral sex. Furthermore, the woman is the one who pays the highest price most of the time. Men can sometimes be foot-loose and fancy-free when it comes to pregnant girlfriends and child-raising. Sexually transmitted diseases can have devastating effects on your health and impact your ability to have a healthy sexual relationship with Mr. Right when he does appear. Too many women have

felt the sinking feeling of suddenly realizing how far-reaching the consequences of one night of careless passion will be as they sit on the doctor's examination table receiving the bad news of their diagnosis. These experiences as well as carrying the burden of knowing you have betrayed your moral principles all create stress, which in turn leads to a myriad of physical ailments.

This generation has seen the rise in popularity of online matchmaking services. While a young (or not-so-young) Lady may agree to meet a virtual stranger in the hope he may turn out to be her knight in shining armor, the unfortunate truth is that at least some of those fellows are on the hunt for an easy target for rape or abuse. Relationships must be built on trust to be healthy and trust is earned over time. Even if your chance of connecting with one of those characters is one in a thousand, is this a risk worth taking?

The U.S. Census Bureau reported the number of forcible rapes committed in this country between 1990 and 2009 was between 75,000 and 86,000 annually. According to the U.S. Department of Justice, a woman is raped every two minutes in America. 57% of rapes have happened on dates. Victims of rape often manifest long-term symptoms of chronic headaches, fatigue, sleep disturbances, recurrent nausea, decreased appetite or eating disorders, menstrual pain, sexual dysfunctions and suicide attempts. These are the excruciating results of a world in rebellion against a loving God who deeply desires to see us choose His ways over ours.

The Gift of Purity

James 1:12 reminds us, *"Happy is the man who doesn't give in and do wrong when he is tempted, for afterwards he will get as his reward the crown of life that God has promised those who love him"* (TLB). The gift of purity, which is a priceless treasure, is to be protected, guarded and honored at all times by the woman *and the man.* Any gentleman worthy of a Lady's affection should care enough about his responsibility to God first, so that he will not put the woman in any errant circumstances. The beauty of a real man shines when he is able to respect a woman's "no" and treat her with love throughout their courtship and even their marriage. Her "no" is not his cue to manipulate her to change her mind in order to get a "yes." If you find yourself challenged or pressured by a man who does not operate by God's commands, it remains your responsibility to yourself and to God to preserve your innocence. One excellent rule of thumb is to avoid the temptation and vulnerability of being alone on your dates. Make your dates a public and supervised occasion.

The Price of Purity

The choice of purity can sometimes result in rejection and dismissal from a relationship, which can cause feelings of deep inadequacy, particularly when exacerbated by others around her misunderstanding the circumstances. Perhaps, he has told outright lies about her or others have simply gossiped or leapt to conclusions. 1Peter 4:4 tells us, *"Of course, your former friends will be very surprised when you don't eagerly join them anymore in the wicked things they do, and they will laugh at you in contempt and scorn"* (TLB). This kind of pain is easier to face if you did not have a sexual relationship that formed a spiritual and emotional bond. You may simply feel sorrow for having to say goodbye to a friend. However, if you were joined together through sex, you may be emotionally devastated, weeping and grief-stricken over the broken relationship. God intended for this level of deep sorrow to be reserved for the man you shared a lifetime with, not a weekend. If you are rejected for your steadfast devotion to God, you're in great company. Jesus Himself experienced such rejection and never once complained.

Sexual Abstinence

According to the Bible, abstinence is God's only policy when it comes to premarital or extramarital sex. Abstinence prevents unwanted pregnancies, aligns relationships with proper spiritual morals, protects babies' lives from abortion, and most importantly, abstinence honors God.

Having sex will undoubtedly change your relationship. Choosing to abstain from sex while dating allows you to know that the person you are dating is with you for YOU! They are not just interested in having sex with you. They respect you and your choices. You will never feel used or exploited for choosing to abstain from sex. If you never wade into the quicksand of sexual promiscuity, you will never know the consequences we've been discussing. Most importantly, did you realize that your pledge to keep yourself pure for the one man God has for you (or perhaps to serve God in chastity for your entire life) will be honored and rewarded by God with eternal benefits?

A Personal Challenge

A Lady's sexual purity is highly important to God. Why wouldn't she have the same regard for herself that God has for her? His rules of respect are in place in the Bible for her protection, safety and covering. A Lady is loved, cherished and esteemed by God.

This chapter has been full of very straightforward talk. I can feel some of you shifting uncomfortably in your chairs and perhaps even holding up your index fingers to object to something we've discussed here. The one anticipated objection that most urgently needs addressing is that many women have already given themselves away sexually and are wondering how in the world they can ever be back in God's grace again. The answer is simple: By the unfathomable work of love Jesus did for you on the cross, there is no past sin, no emotional damage, and no relational wound that cannot be healed and restored. You can make the decision right this minute to conduct the rest of your life by God's standard of purity, ask His forgiveness for your poor choices of the past, be assured you will receive it, and then *"go and sin no more,"* to quote your Savior verbatim. You are never too tarnished to gleam like the precious vessel you are!

So, I present this challenge to all of you, wherever to are on the purity scale: Won't you cherish your virginity and sexual purity like God cherishes it? I appeal to each Lady reading this book to love yourself enough to say, "NO" to sex outside of marriage. Choosing to stay within God's boundaries means that your soul is protected and you are storing up "treasures for yourself in heaven." I promise you won't regret it! If you accept…and I am praying you will…take the pledge on the next page. Read it through and fill in any additional thoughts on the lines provided. Recite it aloud from your heart. Then, sign and date the page to make it official. I would even encourage you to make a copy to keep with your Bible and prayerfully reread it often to help you remain accountable. Try it and see if you don't feel like a true Lady in the court of your King!

A Lady's Pledge of Abstinence

Dear Lord,

Right now, I commit to remaining sexually pure from this day forward. I choose this because I believe that You God, have a plan for my life. I commit my body as a living sacrifice, holy and acceptable unto Christ, which is my act of full worship. I commit myself to turning away from anything that would intentionally or unintentionally lead me away from my commitment to wait [if you are single] or to fidelity [if you are married]. I commit to this goal of purity and abstinence or faithfulness in the plans I make, in the way I choose to dress, in my conversation and speech and with my time. I believe that sex is an incredible gift within the marriage covenant but it can also destroy the lives of those operating outside of Your plan, Lord. I commit to Your foolproof plan of abstinence or faithfulness and my exciting future that is in Your hands as I look to Your provision of my marriage partner. Thank You, God. Amen.

Record any additional thoughts or details you may want to remember as you reread this pledge in the future.

_____

_____

_____

_____

Your Signature

_____

Today's Date

Prayers: A Lady's Sexual Purity

A Prayer For Sexual Purity

Dear Lord,

Make me an instrument of purity. Give me the courage to say "no" at all times, during all situations and under all circumstances to sexual impurity. I want to be pure and holy before You, Lord. I commit to Your Word which tells me that sex outside of marriage is wrong. Help me Lord to do Your will and reap Your benefits of abstinence. In Jesus' Name I Pray. Amen.

A Prayer To Repent From Premarital Sex

Dear Lord,

I admit to You that I have sinned against Your principles of sexual relations outside of wedlock. I ask You to forgive me and to release me from all unrighteousness including all emotional and spiritual ties that I have created through my sin. Thank you for forgiving me and releasing me from all of the repercussions of sexual sins. I repent and turn toward Your will and way for my life. I want to be obedient to Your Word and adhere to Your will. Thank You for healing my heart from all of these relationships and help me to do Your will from here on out. My purity is a matter of respecting myself and trusting You. Help me Lord in both of these areas. In the mighty name of Jesus I pray, Amen.

A Prayer To Repent From Adultery

Dear Lord,

I admit that I have sinned against You, Your will for me and Your Word concerning adultery. I have missed the mark of righteousness and left my covenant promises behind. I ask You to forgive me and to release me from all of my sins and all emotional and spiritual soul-ties that were created because of my sinful choices. I will look to You from this day forward to fulfill me – not for extra-marital affairs to fulfill my life. It is You that I desire and not sexual endeavors, Lord. Release me from all ramifications of sexual encounters outside of my own marriage and heal my broken heart with mercy, grace and moral diligence. Thank You, Lord, for hearing and answering my prayers for my return to righteousness. In Jesus' name I pray, Amen.

Group Discussion: Your Sexual Purity

1. Share your struggles with sexual purity. What pulls at you to indulge or refrain?

2. Have you found yourself saying "yes" to sex when your heart was saying "no"? What did you do in that situation?

3. Do you believe that there is no harm in indulging in sexual activity because you are not harming anyone or yourself? Do you have new or greater understanding of God's reasons for sexual purity?

4. Did you realize that you had as much control as you do in the sexual relationship? Do you have to lead in your relationships? Are you leading because of your own fears or your partner's lack of leadership? Are you ready to surrender your lack of trust and believe that God can handle your life? Why? Why not?

5. Have you broken the ungodly ties with each of your sexual lovers? Do you see a need to be spiritually free from all of these ties that bind to them?

6. What would you like God to do in your life concerning your sexual purity?

*"You did not choose Me, but I chose you
and appointed you that you should go and bear fruit,
and that your fruit should remain,
that whatever you ask the Father in My name
He may give you."
(John 15:16-17)*

❧12❧

HER DECISIONS

A LADY MAKES THE DECISION TO TRUST GOD FOR HER SOLUTIONS.
SHE PLACES HER TRUST IN HIS SCRIPTURAL TRUTH.

Choices, choices, how does a Lady make the right choice? Now that we have studied a Lady's attributes and seen how she can put her life in order through her choice of righteousness, it is time to explore how you can develop the habit of making godly decisions. Let's talk about two contrasting techniques for decision-making you may be using in your everyday life:

1. **The automatic decision making process.**
    This is a decision made without reflection on God's Word—without taking time to think, say a prayer, or ponder the outcome. It is just a quick reaction that is dependent on prior knowledge and a habitual way of addressing an issue. The greatest challenges with automatic responses are, 1) you are not inviting God into your decision-making process, and 2) you are going to get the same results over and over again. When you act without reflecting upon what you are choosing, this is really more of a "reaction" than a "response." For example: Let's say someone pulls in front of your car and cuts you off forcing you to abandon your turn so you must go straight ahead. Your emotional reaction at that time might be to become angry or enraged. You may even yell at the person in the other car. This incident puts you right into the devil's court. And while it is

entirely understandable that you would feel upset, it is important to give your automatic reactions a chance to mellow out into a well thought out, Spirit-led response.

Displaying God's grace and mercy would have been a good response, if you had taken into consideration that the other person might be a stranger to this intersection, have a last minute need to turn, or have another person in the car helping them navigate. In this illustration, you chose to judge the driver through your anger and rage. And when you did, you reflected the nature of the devil, who is always on your perimeter seeking to lure you into sin. By choosing the things of God, like prayer, mercy, grace, and understanding, you could have chosen to exhibit compassion for the other person and perhaps your rush of emotion would have receded faster. Now, I realize that there are times when you should be focusing on your own safety, but with this situation, the factors of faith and touching God were not even considered. This type of auto-reaction omits the spiritual virtues of God in its assumptions. If you don't think or reflect, but just instantly react, you are operating from a worldly standpoint. Having a policy of auto-decision making usually produces poor results and reveals a disconnect from God.

What fruit was produced in the above decision? Let me see. There was self-justification that the other driver was wrong and you were right. There was blame-placing and judgment that you are innocent in your righteous pride and they are guilty. There was anger at others and judgment of their character, and there was the opportunity to openly demonstrate your rage toward others, declaring the injustice done against you. Wow! You have reached the ultimate place of worldly reflection! There is nothing godly about this decision. Good thing this was only a fictional example!

Changing the way you make your choices so they rise to meet the standard of Christ will always produce love, peace, obedience, faithfulness, and all the fruits of God's Spirit. Connecting to the Holy Spirit through faith, will give you the godly outcome you are looking for, so you will be able to keep your peace and foster a right relationship with God. Your soul will stay calm and so will your attitude of righteousness.

2. The time-out decision making process.

This type of decision making invites the Lord into your situation. The "time-out" process is where you extend an "invitation" to the Lord to enter into your situation. It requires making an intentional connection to Him by faith, "praying" about your circumstance and seeking Him for help to support you and bring you to a prosperous outcome and place of peace. This can be done by taking a time-out in your mind, especially if you are in front of someone and can't take time to step away to pray. Sometimes though, this time-out may be an actual stepping away into a quiet place to have a moment with God. Either way of taking a time-out will give you a moment to invite God into your decision-making process. Your moment of reflection to ask for help means that you are seeking *His* guidance, you need *His* help and your dependence on Him says that only *He* can handle this situation—you are not capable of making a godly decision alone. Therefore, God is not excluded as in the automatic decision-making process, rather whole-heartedly invited to give you a complete response to your needs.

Regardless of the amount of time you have to make a decision, your process should include two elements. *First,* the extending of a prayer of petition to God, meaning a request for His help, and *second,* a personal and heartfelt invitation to enter into your situation so the outcome will be His way and not yours. God wants to be that immediate and automatic part of your life every waking moment. He wants to be the one that you turn to each time. Therefore, asserting your faith by inviting Him into your circumstance requires a prayer and an invitation to ask Him to *save* you in this moment, acknowledging that only He can do this for you.

The Process of Making Choices

Making new choices means you will have to be trusting with full faith that God will provide a way for you to succeed. You will also need to have the knowledge of "What Would Jesus Do" in any situation and you will want to know what it will cost to make a different choice. In order to move forward in growth and maturity you will want to make your decisions based on biblical principles. To help you get started on this path here are three pillars on which to build your decision-making policy.

1. **Trust God with Faith**

    Applying your faith is the first key to making choices. Hebrews 11:1 says, *"Faith is the substance of things hoped for, the evidence of things not seen."* Faith means that you are trusting in something that you can't see quite yet but you are confident that it will come. Faith is the response that God is looking for from each of us. We can't always see the road ahead but if we trust in *Who* is leading us down the road, we will surely arrive safe and sound at our destiny. God wants us to trust in Him whether we can see around the next bend or not. That trust involves a decision to obey and follow, regardless of what things we may see with our natural vision. You are not trusting in your own strength to see around the next corner, rather you are engaging in willingness to be led by God's love, mercy, and will. Can you trust Him to lead you ahead without knowing the next encounter or contriving the next choice yourself?

2. **Consider: What Would Jesus Do?**

    When we read the gospels, we can clearly see that each time Jesus faced a choice, His decision was to please His Heavenly Father. For us, emotional choices may take us down the path that leads to anger and outbursts, while solely intellectual choices require that we independently come up with the perfect solution to our problems—no God needed! However, there is an option that many people do not consider: **the spiritual choice!** What does it require? Indulging in relationship with Jesus, knowing who He is and what His choices would be. When we know Him, we will understand why He did what He did and what made Him choose what He did. The Bible tells us that He only did what the Father told Him to do. Do you think that you could begin to listen to God in this same fashion and follow Him directly? "It would be pretty hard," you say? Yes, for a while until you became used to connecting to God and hearing His responses. Hearing and (more importantly) listening, then following obediently what His Word instructs is what we as Christians are required to do. We are to learn the living Word so excellently that we will want to obey it, follow it, trust it and believe it in our decision-making process.

"What Would Jesus Do" is the same thing that we are supposed to be doing. This includes trusting Him, developing an open relationship with Him, reading His Word, believing in Jesus' death, resurrection and life, praying moment by moment, and telling others of the Good News of the Gospel. Doing what Jesus did means leading an active Christ-like life. It is, in a very real way, sharing the same life that Jesus had while here on earth. Living this way, when decisions and choices need to be made, you will look to the ways of Christ and the Bible as your reference and guide. Discovering what "Jesus Would Do" is a lifetime journey of study and biblical research which will lead you into an ever-deepening relationship with Him. That, Ladies, is a joy, not a chore!

3. **Count The Cost of Your Decision**

We know that all of us are called upon to make hundreds of choices every day. Some choices have no clear right or wrong direction. We are able to make some hasty choices without fear of retribution or regrets. However, there are many more choices that come with deep consequences that we will have to face if we make the wrong decision. The Bible tells us to count the cost when we consider implementing new ways. Luke 14:28 *"For which of you, intending to build a tower, does not sit down first and count the cost, whether he has enough to finish it."* Please know that when you start an endeavor you must consider whether you have what you need to finish the task you started. In this Scripture, Jesus was telling the disciples that if they wished to follow Him that they would have to carry their own cross throughout their discipleship journey. This meant that on some occasions, the cross might seem overwhelming to carry because of the heaviness of the task. Nevertheless, it was their responsibility to endure the experience.

Many people quit in the middle of their pursuits because they did not count the cost from the beginning, nor are they willing to take responsibility for carrying their own cross all the way through to completion. Sometimes their soulish junk needs to be weeded out and discarded because that is what is making the load too heavy to carry. Their minds need to be renewed (Rom 12:2) and they need to cast down all imaginations as in 2 Corinthians 10:5-6 which says, *"Casting down arguments and every high thing that exalts itself against the knowledge of God, bringing every thought into captivity to the obedience of Christ."* We are to be responsible for our own load says Galatians 6:5 *"Each of us must bear some faults and burdens of his own. For none of us is perfect"* (TLB)! Therefore as we journey in our endeavors we need to count the cost of continuing to carry our own soulish baggage. A good soul cleaning, through confession, forgiveness and repentance, does wonders to restore our lives.

When counting your cost, there are some key things you will want to carefully weigh:

♥ **The cost of staying with the original choice.**
This is making the decision to stay the course and ride it out, neither adding or subtracting anything from what you are doing presently. The pain that is connected with this option is usually depression because you are deny-ing that you have to make a decision or that a decision can be considered to change your circumstances. There-fore, you have to face the same old thing again and again, every day. No change is on the horizon.

For example, you know that you should relinquish your anger, unforgiveness and judgment against someone but you decide that you are not going to. The cost is: You are oh-so-willing to go around the mount-ain again and again, content to ignore any new options which may become available. The price you will be paying over and over again is your inability to come into God's presence with this garbage. He wants the baggage left at the door of His garden. Your spiritual growth will slow down because you will not be hearing from God as easily as you heard before nor will you experience the production of good spiritual fruit in your life through obedience to the Word of God. You also will not be planting any seeds of growth into other's lives because you can't give what you don't have. If God is the only thing on this earth that is love, then how will you give love when you make a choice to exclude God? 1 John 4:16 reminds us that, *"God is love, and anyone who lives in love is living with God and God is living in him"* (TLB).

♥ **The cost of indecisiveness.**

This is still a choice but you are not moving forward, rather wavering in your conviction that a decision needs to be made. Inside, this hurts just as much as staying in the original choice because you are stalling a decision that needs to be made. You will reap the same harvest as you would making no decision at all. Most of the time, fear of making the wrong choice keeps us bound and indecisive. It seems safer to stay undecided because you will not have to face failure. Failure, you believe, shows everyone how inadequate you are.

Just as in the first example, you carry anger, unforgiveness and judgment against someone only this time, you may not be so content to let these feelings stand, but you push the discomfort down. You see the need for the decision but you choose to stay indecisive, putting off the new possibility in front of you. Everything in your heart is walking in unwillingness, which is *status quo* and the blinders are firmly on your eyes. You have even turned up the music and plugged in your ear buds! The cost of indecisiveness is similar to deliberately sticking with your original choice because you are hindering God from helping you mature, and prosper. In effect, the life you were created for is passing you by while you refuse to make the decision to move forward.

♥ **The cost if you move forward in a new choice.**
Making a new choice may require some transition time and involve some discomfort as you encounter new situations, but carries with it the hope of new and better results. This method can be challenging if you're usually adverse to change. In your heart, you know that you want to relinquish your anger, unforgiveness and any judgment you may be holding against someone. So, you make the decision to move forward in obedience to God. The price of a godly choice is well worth paying. It will cost you precisely the weight of the garbage you were carrying on your back and your out-of-sorts position with God. It will also pay out dividends in your transformed, renewed countenance and the fruit you bear. You will find yourself in right relationship with God, so His anointing will be upon you.

Here is a quick list of personal questions you can ask yourself whenever you are faced with a choice.
- ♥ Will my choice glorify God? (1Cor10:31)
- ♥ Will my choice help me to do my best in life? (1 Cor 9:25)
- ♥ Will my choice harm others in any way? (1 Cor 9:20-23)
- ♥ Will my choice cause me or others to sin? (1 Cor 10:32)
- ♥ Will my choice be the best action to take for myself? (1 Cor 10:23, 33)
- ♥ Will my choice be selfish or unloving? (1 Cor 10:28-31)
- ♥ Will my choice motivate others to know Christ? (1 Cor 10:33)
- ♥ Will my choice help my witness and testimony for Christ? (1Cor 19:19-22)

If you are asking and praying about these questions and you are reading the accompanying Scriptures regularly, then you can nearly always reap the benefit of hearing God's voice for your circumstances. Remember, you can't get too far off of God's track because He has you covered with His grace and mercy. So try your wings, begin to invite God into your situation and enjoy the journey.

How Can I Know I Am Following God's Will?

Many ask, "How do I know God's will?" There is no magic formula except to know God's character and nature by studying what He has revealed about Himself. When you meet someone new, the only way to get to know them is to spend time with them, right? Spending time with God reading His Word, listening to His Holy Spirit, and then trusting Him by applying His teachings to your life will give you a greater knowledge and understanding of Him. The more you do this, the more you will find yourself wanting to walk in obedience to what you have learned.

God simply wants us to learn to take one step each day. Don't steal, or cheat, don't curse, don't be jealous over what others have, don't kill, and honor Him on the Sabbath are the simple acts of obedience of doing God's will. If you can accomplish the basics then God will show you more.

Many Ladies are raising families while also actively involved in church ministries. Some of you may feel you are called overseas to the mission fields of Africa or China. But, be sure to attend to your families first, before laying down your life for a good cause or another's benefit, because God has told us clearly that this is His will. He gave you your first responsibility of raising a family. If you can add to that responsibility with more duties without neglecting the primary one then have at it. Some of us think it would be nice to leave behind the ho-hum life and take up an exciting mission. However, if you struggle with maintaining obedience to God in your daily routine, how will you ever be obedient in any other setting?

Making the decision to find the truth of God's Word is an excellent start for being in God's will. Digesting the New Testament, Psalms and Proverbs can bring great wisdom and understanding to your decision-making process and can facilitate growth and maturity in your walk with Christ. Communicating with God through daily prayer, worshiping Him in song, praise and thankfulness, perhaps even dancing before Him in worship like King David did will usher you into His presence and connect your heart with His. The first priority in a Lady's daily decision-making process is to learn to connect with God, in doing so, you will be able to know, hear and understand God's will for your life in all of the decisions that must be made.

Sweet Lady, don't fret about making a mistake or making an incorrect decision. Whatever choices you make, your God is always there to partner with you, if you will just allow Him in. He knows where you are and understands what it will take to move you along the path He chose for you before you were born. Your part is to simply live out your faith in Him at all times. You have His direct promise that He will never leave you or forsake you, that He is right here with you forever and ever (Deu 31:6).

Prayer: Making Choices

Dear Lord,

Making decisions based on Your truth is important to You so I too embrace the importance of making the right choice in decision-making for my life. I acknowledge the godly choice of Your will always, proving to align itself with Your Holy Word and giving me revelation and life abundantly. Therefore, I ask You to forgive me for not incorporating the truth of Your Word into my daily practice of decision-making. I have eliminated You in all of my ways. I choose to forgive myself for all of my poor choices and to lay down all guilt and shame connected with all of my failures and shortcomings when making my choices.

I ask You to help me to quickly obey the conviction of the Holy Spirit to move me in the direction of Your will at all times. I put away all embarrassments caused when becoming intimate with You in decision-making. Assist me to enjoy my time in prayer with You, worshiping and praising You in song and dance as I begin to make good decisions before You as my new decisions in You begin to flow .

Come live in my heart and guide me always, Lord. Open up my understanding of You, Lord Jesus, and help me to see Your way as my only choice in decisions. I want to do things Your way and embrace obedience as my life-line to all of my decisions. Help Lord, help to move me forward in You! In the mighty name of Jesus I pray. Amen.

Group Discussion: Making Decisions

1. What are some of your challenges with making decisions? Share with the group your defeats and victories.

2. Are you asserting God's will in your decisions and choices? Do you align your decision process with spiritual truth? How?

3. What choices or decisions have you made that you would do differently today if you had to make those choices again? Why ?

4. Share your challenges of walking the virtuous life of a Lady?

5. Do you struggle with the basic elements of being a Christian, like bible reading time, prayer time, worship time, confession, repentance, forgiveness, connecting to God as your Heavenly Father, and believing that you are forgiven? Which of these are your greatest struggles?

6. Are you willing to commit to a deeper spiritual walk with God? Why? Why not? In what ways will you commit?

A Lady's Prayer

Dear Beloved Lord Jesus,

I desire to be the Lady You created me to be. I want all that You have for me, Lord. I ask that You bring forth Your love and provision, never ceasing to amaze me or show off for me. I come near to worship and commune with You this day to proclaim again my desire to follow You with all my heart. Help me to develop into Your divine image of the Christ that lives in me. I ask for Your measure of **commitment** to be placed in me. I only seek Your level of devotedness and dedicate myself to You, pledging my life to you Lord and choosing to believe with all my heart that You are Lord of all.

I ask also for Your measure of **esteem** that I no longer would despise myself but know that I am accepted as Your beloved at all times and forever. You are my God and I am Your Lady. I thank You for Your **character** and **identity** in me that is continually being expanded and sanctified. I only want Your image to shine through my heart, bringing revelation and enlightenment of who You really are. I receive Your righteousness as the unmerited favor of Your grace in my true identity.

Help me to present my **prayers** to You Lord, as a sweet smelling aroma to Your nostrils as You breathe in every breath and return to me Your favor. I long to touch You with my worship and praise, and desire that You hear my every need and answer my every petition with Your will.

Help me also Lord, to choose **purity** as my sustaining choice at all times. I am weak in my flesh and need Your help. Provide strength for me to say "no" so that I might preserve my body for marriage as Your Word commands. When I am joined through marriage I ask You to help me to stay faithful to the covenant I have vowed with my words and with my heart.

I petition you for Your guidance in the righteousness of my **integrity**. Help me to be honest with myself and open with my responses to others. Lord, thank You also for drawing me to the decision of **salvation**. It comforts me to know that Jesus is my Savior. I desire Your salvation provision to work in my life always and forever.

Help me Lord to manage my **emotions**. My feelings want to lead me at times but with Your help, I will succeed at responding with Your will and not my own unbalanced feelings.

Thank You, Lord, for Your total **forgiveness** of all my sins. You have thrown my sins into the Sea of Forgetfulness. Convict me to follow your commands to forgive others and give me strength when I am called to do so. I desire to forgive with swiftness and joy to release others and myself from indebtedness that we can't repay.

I acknowledge that you have created me to be Your special Lady. Thank You for fashioning me with Your eternal purposes in mind. I shall cherish my **femininity** as a gift from You forever.

Aid me, Lord, to make godly **decisions** from this day forward. I need Your guidance continually. I invite You into my situations and give You permission to lead me in the path of righteousness. I ask You to hear this prayer and to work in it continually for my benefit. In the mighty name of Jesus I pray. Amen!

APPENDIX A

STARTING YOUR SMALL GROUP

These instructions will help you put together a group focused on recovering from broken-heartedness and on developing the capacity to repent, forgive, and be accountable. It isn't always easy or appropriate to try to create a group environment like this without a trained facilitator leading the way, particularly if you are dealing with issues like addiction, abuse, mental or physical illness. I'm sharing with you here the methodology I use with my small support groups, where I have personally trained a number of people to facilitate by these guidelines. So, this section won't read like an instruction sheet for a simple ladies bible study. I'm presuming you're reading this because you feel called and prepared to step into the leadership role in such a group. If you feel over your head, I encourage you to approach a counselor or trained facilitator to help your group navigate these waters. The experience can be extremely rewarding if done responsibly. Of course, neither this book nor this group format is intended to replace appropriate medical or psychological care, should that be appropriate for any individual. This is an agreement among functioning Ladies who wish to explore their options for healing and spiritual growth in a safe environment.

Gather together a small group (ideally) 6-8 women, who are interested in learning to discuss their spiritual walk and be accountable to each other. Plan to meet once a week for 12 weeks in a place where you can comfortably discuss your experience with reading this book and your answers to the discussion questions. Start each meeting with an opening prayer and thank God for His presence as you gather in His name. Then, review the assigned chapter with the group for about 15 minutes. You may also assign the review segment to a different Lady each week. Allow about 10 minutes for each Lady to share her discussion question responses. Ask them to answer from their hearts and to share their feelings as openly as they are comfortable.

End the group time by inviting your Ladies to offer their prayer requests and asking them to make notes so they can pray for each other throughout the week. Spend a few moments allowing each group member to take a turn to pray for another Lady. As the leader, you will close the meeting in corporate prayer and assign the next chapter to read and answer the discussion questions before gathering together the next time.

The Object Of The Group

Submission to the work of the Holy Spirit during group time is each Lady's objective. Confession or sharing what is in the deepest crevices of their hearts helps prompt a spirit of forgiveness and repentance which, in turn, brings about freedom and release from carrying secret burdens. This kind of restoration promotes a wholeness of spiritual character and a noticeable Christ-likeness which achieves the goal of the Holy Spirit.

The Commitment To The Group

The first purpose of commitment among your group members is to ensure that the individuals are in unity and the group is functioning optimally. Without commitment to guidelines, the group cannot be in one accord. The second purpose is to create a sense of ownership among the members. Ownership means that as you care, nurture and develop your investment in the group, you will reap a return on something that you own. As planting brings a harvest, you will grow a crop. Each Lady will actually walk away with something more than she arrived with. As each one honors their commitment, the Ladies in your group will bond in a deep and lasting way and everyone will receive the maximum benefit from the shared experience.

If you are leading the group, it's also a good idea to collect contact information for each Lady, such as their cell phone number and email address, whether or not they use text messaging, and the best time to reach them. I suggest asking for emergency contact information to keep on record as well. Track attendance to help you hold your Ladies accountable. If someone in the group does not seem able to keep their commitment, you may suggest, in love, that they consider stepping out of the group so the others can continue without disruption.

By signing the pledge on the next page, each group member formalizes their commitment to the group and agrees to abide by and uphold the rules for the benefit of themselves and all other group members. Please feel free to make copies of the pledge or type it up for your own use.

MY PLEDGE TO THIS GROUP

I agree to attend all 12 meetings. I will be prompt in arriving, and committing myself to attending for the entire duration of the program.

I agree to uphold CONFIDENTIALITY. I understand keeping confidences adds safety and emotional stability to the group. Information shared by others in this group does not belong to me and is not mine to share with others. I shall only share my own information in and out of the group.

I agree not to share the member's names who attend the group meetings with anyone.

I agree to submit to the purpose of the support group. Gaining holy revelation and applying the principles of God's truth to my life is my goal; not simply acquiring head knowledge.

I agree to be open and honest about my own feelings and emotions. I am to actively participate with God in the process of healing. I determine to discover my feelings, repent, forgive and release my anxiety to God.

I agree to be patient and supportive with all group members. I will not try to give advice or pressure other group members to do what I think is best. I will encourage them to share their experiences openly, and to trust and believe that God will provide all that is necessary for them to heal.

I agree to do the homework each week. I need the insight that it gives me as I seek God's will and help in my life.

Signed: _____

Date: _____

How To Talk In A Support Group

Speaking in "I" statements can help clarify and distinguish you from another person. It is not a crime to say "I." It can even be valuable and loving to reveal the truth about your thoughts, beliefs, attitudes, opinions and feelings to others. It is often very courageous and considerate to let someone else discover your innermost self. Psalms 73:16 says, *"When I thought how to understand this, it was too painful for me."*

Avoiding "You" Statements.

♥ "You" statements put others at a distance, identifying them instead of yourself.

♥ "You" statements hide yourself so others can't see you as the one with the issue.

♥ "You" statements keep you from getting in touch with your own feelings, opinions, thinking and issues.

Sharing With "I" Statements

♥ Use "I" statements to refocus on your own issues and not others'.

♥ Use "I" statements to be honest with yourself about the truth of your heart.

♥ Use "I" statements to help you identify and express your own feelings.

"You" Statements	"I" Statements
"You are so embarrassing when you do that."	"I feel so embarrassed when you do that. "
"You aren't taking good enough care of my things."	"I need more care with my things than you are giving."
"You keep me from achieving my goals."	"I can't achieve my goals when I am with you."
"You know how when you feel sad, you don't want to leave the house?"	"I don't feel like leaving the house when I am feeling sad."
"You ruined everything!"	"I felt the situation was ruined when you did that."

The Group's Responsibilities

♥ To support each member as they get in touch with their feelings and share from their hearts.

♥ To offer understanding, while the members adjust to exposing their issues in the group setting.

♥ To validate the members feelings with words of affirmation.

♥ To be brief when sharing. Get to the point, try not to repeat yourself or ramble on tangents.

♥ To limit the details. Give a quick summary. Dwelling on details can be a defense mechanism to hide out, keeping you from the real issue.

♥ To be considerate of other's sharing time. All members need a chance to speak.

Focus On How You Feel Or Felt About A Situation.

♥ Listen to what you are telling yourself concerning the "feelings" of the issue. Try to identify them. They belong to you. Then give yourself permission to "feel" your feelings.

♥ Express your feelings. A release of power takes place, as you express your feelings and the root of the issue is exposed. You will gain a new perspective simply by hearing your own pain. Then healing can take place.

When Listening In The Group

♥ Listen to what the talker is saying.

♥ Be sensitive to their feelings while being aware of your own emotional reactions.

♥ Don't interrupt them.

♥ Reflect back your summary of what you heard them say. Then allow them to clarify your feedback.

♥ Ask if they have more to share.

- ♥ Use validation as your response: "That was brave of you to share." "Thank you for sharing from your heart."
- ♥ Use affirmation to continue to validate their pain as being real. "I hear your pain. That must have been a terrible experience."

Let God Be the Healer of Your Wounds

- ♥ God is the one who heals your wounds. We are not the "fixer" or healer. Don't assume this heavy role.
- ♥ Statements of conclusion that imply "fixing others" are not permitted. Example: "I know what you can do." "Did you try this_____?" "I had that experience and I did this _____." These statements do not help members seek God's revelation about their healing.
- ♥ Do not fix, analyze, judge, counsel, vent, cross talk, give statements of conclusion, your opinion or your testimony of goodness. Leave these to the professionals.

Additional Help

Be open to seeking additional coaching or counseling and keep in mind that resolution and reconciliation of the heart takes time, energy, love and patience.

APPENDIX B

BREAKING SOUL-TIES

A soul-tie is a bonding together of two people's souls, meaning their mind, will and emotions. The Bible talks about two souls being knit together and becoming one flesh. *"For this reason a man shall leave his father and mother and be joined to his wife, and the two shall become one flesh. So then, they are no longer two but one flesh. Therefore what God has joined together, let not man separate"* (Matt 19:5-6).

A soul-tie in its simplest form in marriage is when the soul draws each partner together forming a bond, so that the pair is operating as one. The two are in agreement together, walking according to one flesh and the godly tie between the husband and wife is intended by God to be an unbreakable bond by man (Mark 10:7-9).

However, in sexual relations when not in a marital agreement an ungodly soul-tie is formed by the couple which gnaws and pulls in a negative and counter-productive way. This soul-tie causes wreckage and waste to the soul, and is destructive. 1 Corinthians 6:15-17 *"Do you not know that your bodies are members of Christ? Shall I then take the members of Christ and make them members of a harlot? Certainly not! Or do you not know that he who is joined to a harlot is one body with her? For 'the two,' He says, 'shall become one flesh.' But he who is joined to the Lord is one spirit with Him."*

People who have had many relationships find it very difficult to bond or be joined to anyone beyond their sexual affairs, because their soul is so divided and fragmented. The Word continues in 1 Corinthians 6:18-20 to desperately warn us, *"Flee sexual immorality! Every sin that a man does is outside the body, but he who commits sexual immorality sins against his own body. Or do you not know that your body is the temple of the Holy Spirit who is in you, whom you have from God, and you are not your own? For you were bought at a price; therefore glorify God in your body and in your spirit, which are God's."*

Symptoms of Ungodly Soul-ties

- ♥ Obsessive preoccupation with another, to the neglect of the things of the Lord.
- ♥ Tendencies to be domineering and controlling or passive and apathetic in a relationship.
- ♥ Inability to truly forgive from the heart.
- ♥ Another person's voice playing over and over in the mind like a tape-recorder.
- ♥ Inability to bring a relationship under godly order and control of the Holy Spirit.
- ♥ Patterns of anger, blame and accusations in a relationship.
- ♥ Fear of "being real with" or speaking truth to another.
- ♥ Psychic or occult phenomena within a relationship.

How to Break a Soul-tie

1. Repent of committing the sin of fornication or adultery. These form horrible soul-ties drawing the two of you together continually even when you have separated and gone on to another relationship.

2. If gifts were given to you in connection with the unholy relationship, get rid of them! Such things as rings symbolize the ungodly relationship, and can hold a soul-tie in place. Also all items given during an adulterous affair should be destroyed like flowers and love letters.

3. Break any rash vows, agreements or commitments made to the other person (Numbers 30:2). These play a part in forming the soul-tie and should be confessed, renounced, repented of, and broken in Jesus' name. Even words like "I will love you forever" or "I could never love another man" need to be renounced. These spoken commitments need to be undone verbally as Proverbs 21:23 tells us, *"Whoever guards his mouth and*

his tongue keeps his soul from troubles." The tongue has the ability to bring the soul into great bondage and devastation.

4. Forgive yourself for being foolish, agreeing to indulge in sex, for rebelling against God's commandments and enticing the other person into sinning. Also, forgive the other person for alluring you into sin and betraying their loyalties to God and disrespecting you.

5. Renounce the soul-tie by professing this prayer from your heart:

Dear Heavenly Father,

In the Name of Jesus, I submit my soul, my desires and my emotions to You. I confess to you all my ungodly mind, will, emotions and body ties as sin. I choose to forgive all my sexual partners involved (name the people) and I ask You to forgive me for my participation in this sin that resulted in ungodly ties. I choose to forgive myself for all my fleshly indulgences in sex outside of marriage or in an adulterous affair. I renounce and break all evil spirits that have been associated with these ungodly soul-ties right now and I break every vow, commitment and agreement I have made with these sexual partners.

Father, I loose myself from all relationships that are not ordained by You and I surrender my flesh to You in submission to your holy Word. I break all ties emotionally, intellectually, physically, spiritually, and all ties based on domination, manipulations, control, fornication, adultery, lust and deception. (Numbers 30:2)

Holy Lord, help me to set aside all sexually illicit or illegitimate unions so I may freely give my soul to

You, Lord. I ask that You cleanse me from all of my unrighteousness and set my soul free from turning to these sins again. I ask that You command your angels to retrieve all of the fragmented pieces of my soul and return them to their original position.

Finally, in the name of Jesus, I declare every demonic hold that has come as a result of these ungodly soul-ties, to be rendered null and void. Satan, I renounce you and your demons and command you to depart from my spirit, soul and body right now!" Lord, I thank You for forgiving all of my sins and I receive Your forgiveness into my heart. I give You all the glory for my holiness for now, I am a prisoner of the Lord's, beseeching to walk worthy of the vocation where I have been called, with all lowliness and meekness, with long-suffering, forbearing with others in agape love. I endeavor to keep the unity of the Spirit in the bond of peace with Christ. (Eph. 4:1-3) In Jesus name I pray. Amen

NOTES

[1] Neil Anderson, *Christ Centered Therapy* (Grand Rapids: Zondervan, 2000), 94-95.

[2] The word "integrity" is translated from the Hebrew *"tōm,"* which means uprightness, perfection, and moral innocence.
Strong's Exhaustive Concordance of The Bible (Nashville: Thomas Nelson, 1990).

[3] *The Open Bible, Study Edition* (Nashville: Thomas Nelson, 1990), 1494.

[4] June Hunt, *Counseling Through Your Bible Handbook* (Eugene: Harvest House, 2008) 376-377.

[5] The concept of soul-ties is drawn from *Seductions Exposed, The Spiritual Dynamics of Relationships* by Dr. Gary L. Greenwald (Irvine, Eagles Nest, 1988).

[6] 1 Corinthians 11:3 [And the head of the woman is the man] "The sense is, she is subordinate to him, and in all circumstances—in her demeanor, her dress, her conversation, in public and in the family circle—should recognize her subordination to him. The particular thing here referred to is, that if the woman is inspired, and speaks or prays in public, she should by no means lay aside the usual and proper symbols of her subordination." From *Barnes' Notes, Electronic Database*. Copyright 1997 by Biblesoft.

PHOTOGRAPHY CREDITS

The photographs on pages 26, 34, 38, 73, 76, 89, 105, 117, 148, 161, and 164 are by Michelle Arnold.
Foto by Michelle
http://www.fotobymichelle.com

The photographs on pages 11, 120, 131 and on the "About the Authors" page are by Jeannie Capellan.
Jeannie Capellan Photography
http://jeanniecapellan.com

The photograph on page 51 is by Lynn Erhorn.

The photograph on page 61 is by Deidra Lazard.

ABOUT THE AUTHORS

Dr. Joyce Shelton and Lynn Erhorn minister the gospel of Jesus Christ in the greater Jacksonville, Florida area. Their ministries are devoted to counseling and coaching those God places in their care to their fullest potential, physically, emotionally, and spiritually. This is their first book together, although they spend precious time sitting in sand chairs at the ocean's edge planning their next one. They are grateful to God for each other, for the fire in their hearts, and for their families who have supported them through this writing process and in every other way.